FELBRIGG HALL

Norfolk

John Maddison

THE NATIONAL TRUST

Acknowledgements

No English house has been described with greater knowledge and affection than the subject of Wyndham Ketton-Cremer's beautifully written *Felbrigg: The Story of a House*. This much shorter book is intended as a useful guide to the property, which may also serve as a tangible record of a visit to Felbrigg. It leans heavily upon the Squire's account and supplements it only in its greater preoccupation with bricks and mortar, with inventories and objects, and with the story that they tell.

I am much indebted to a number of people who have given freely of their knowledge of Felbrigg. The guidebook of 1980 written by Gervase Jackson-Stops and his subsequent comments on my text have been indispensable. The picture entries have been written by Alastair Laing. Joan Thomas has put at my disposal her extensive notes and I have learnt much from David Musson, who was the Trust's first managing agent for Felbrigg, and from Ted Bullock, the Head Gardener since 1970. Elizabeth Griffiths's thesis on the early history of the estate was especially useful to me, as was John Phibbs's history of the landscape, and I have had many enlightening conversations with Nicolas de Bazille Corbin, the former Regional Agent for East Anglia, and with Merlin Waterson. Marjorie Rhodes kindly made available her BA dissertation on the architectural history of Felbrigg. My task would have been impossible without the assistance of the staff at the Norfolk and Norwich Record Office. Graham Hicks, Jim Watts and the house staff at Felbrigg have also been consistently helpful, as have David Adshead and Ann den Engelse at the East Anglia Regional Office. I am grateful to Jim Marshall for reading and revising the chapter on the garden. The Trust would also like to thank the following: Joanna Barnes, Gary Battell, Dr William Cole, Sir Brinsley Ford, Dr John Ingamells, Heidrun Jecht, Scilla Langdale, Phoebe Lowry, Sir Oliver Millar, Michael Robinson, Dr Malcolm Rogers, the Marquess of Townshend.

John Maddison

Photographs: Geremy Butler pp. 14, 21, 83 (right); Nicolette Hallett p. 15; National Monuments Record p. 87; National Trust pp. 24, 28, 34, 46, 50, 58, 91, 93; National Trust Photographic Library/Oliver Benn p. 1; NTPL/John Hammond pp. 13, 17, 19, 23, 27, 28, 31, 35, 45, 53, 55, 61, 75; NTPL/Nadia MacKenzie front cover, pp. 16, 25, 32, 49, 52, 65, 67, 68, 72, 78, 79, back cover; NTPL/Marianne Majerus p. 83 (top and middle left); NTPL/Brian Middlehurst p. 22; NTPL/Rupert Truman pp. 4, 9, 10, 20, 38, 84, 86; Norfolk Museums Service, Todd collection p. 89; Society of Antiquaries of London p. 7.

First published in Great Britain in 1995 by the National Trust
© 1995 The National Trust
Registered charity no. 205846
ISBN 0 7078 0220 2

Designed by James Shurmer

Phototypeset in Monotype Bembo Series 270
by Southern Positives and Negatives (SPAN), Lingfield, Surrey (9721)

Printed in Great Britain by Balding + Mansell
for National Trust Enterprises Ltd, 36 Queen Anne's Gate, London SW1H 9AS

CONTENTS

The south front

INTRODUCTION

It is not possible to look at the Jacobean south front of Felbrigg for more than a few minutes without being struck by the extraordinary disparity of its fabric. The Norfolk weather has torn and scratched at its ancient surface, revealing not only the successive decorations of past owners but good and bad repairs, and great sections of wall made up of widely differing materials: brick, plaster, pebbles, flints, rusting iron and wonderfully wrought limestone. Here is human geology; an appealing mixture of man and nature in which the natural elements seem gradually to be getting the upper hand. The Jacobean mason with his pattern-book classicism and his deep attachment to the mullioned oriels of the Gothic past touches us with his sincerity. But if we walk round to the south-west corner, we are suddenly confronted by the immaculate brick façade of the 1680s 'New Appartment' standing like an entirely different house. A cultivated and cosmopolitan product of the Restoration, it ostentatiously ignores its slightly dishevelled elderly relative and stares resolutely across the ha-ha. This is a house of surprising contrasts and strong characters.

The south front is the house built by Sir John Wyndham for his son Thomas and was formed out of the carcass of an early Tudor building. The Norfolk Windhams (who had only recently begun to spell their name with an 'i') had been here since the estate passed out of the hands of the Felbrigg family in the mid-fifteenth century, but when their line died out in 1599, the Somerset Wyndhams took over, reasserting the family presence with the construction of the new front in 1621–4 and adopting the Norfolk spelling.

It was Thomas Windham's son William I who dramatically extended the Jacobean house with the new red-brick west wing in the 1680s, employing the virtuoso William Samwell as his architect and decorating its interiors with wonderful plaster-work, but neither architect nor patron lived to see its completion. The new squire, Ashe Windham, who succeeded in 1689, built the Orangery and the new service courtyard on the east side of the house in the early eighteenth century. He also completed the interior of the west wing, but his work and that of his father was to be altered and much enriched by William Windham II, who returned from an extensive and eventful Grand Tour in 1742, weighed down with books and pictures. On Ashe's death in 1749 William engaged the architect James Paine to refashion the interiors to accommodate his new possessions, and to put up a new east service wing. Paine's Rococo rooms are amongst the most satisfying of their period and were little altered after William Windham's early death in 1761. His son, the great politician William Windham III, died without heirs leaving the estate to Vice-Admiral William Lukin, the son of his half-brother. Lukin was required to change his name to Windham, and in 1824 he employed W. J. Donthorn to remodel Paine's service wing with Gothic windows and to build a new neo-Tudor stable block. The alteration of the Great Hall by his son William Howe Windham in the early 1840s was the last significant architectural change at Felbrigg. In spite of Felbrigg's rapid decline during the period of the eccentric spendthrift 'Mad Windham', who inherited in 1854, its sale to John Ketton in 1863, and a period of unchecked decay at the beginning of this century, the house and its contents survived substantially intact. The Ketton-Cremer family, to whom the estate passed in 1923, were descended from the Somerset Wyndhams. They set about the gradual repair of a very rundown establishment in spite of limited means. Robert Wyndham Ketton-Cremer carried on this work, devoting himself to Felbrigg. When he died in 1969, he left the estate, the house and its contents to the National Trust.

CHAPTER ONE
EARLY HISTORY

It is three miles from Cromer, delightfully situated in the bosom of extensive and venerable woods. The oak, the beech and the Spanish chesnut seem congenial to the soil; and the form of the ground, which consists of gently rising hills and vales, is admirably constituted to shew to the greatest advantage the masses of light and shade produced by such a combination.[1]

The name is a relic of the Danish invasions: *Fiolbrygga* is ancient Scandinavian for a plank bridge. When the Norman invaders made their Domesday survey in 1086, the village was amongst the many possessions of the Bigod family and had presumably been so since the ejection of two freemen of Harold's brother Gyrth. The earliest record of a family taking Felbrigg as its name comes from the late eleventh century when Ailward de Felbrigg and his kinsmen were joined by marriage to the Bigods. In the chancel of St Margaret's church, which stands in the park to the south of the house, is a monumental brass which is unusual in depicting two successive lords of the manor and their wives. The first, Simon de Felbrigg, is thought to have died in 1351 and is shown with his wife Alice de Thorp. Next to them, in armour, is their son Roger and his wife Elizabeth, daughter of Lord Scales. Roger was a soldier who fought in France in the 1350s and was one of the earliest of Felbrigg's many owners to travel extensively abroad.

The brass was probably laid by Roger's famous son, Sir Simon Felbrigg, who had been born in about 1366 and was to follow in his father's footsteps, joining the service of John of Gaunt and fighting alongside him and other Norfolk knights in France and Spain. By 1394 he had found a place at the court of Richard II and was described as a 'king's knight'. A year later he was made royal standard bearer with an annual payment of £100. Other perquisites followed, notably the keeperships

of certain royal castles including the old Bigod stronghold of Framlingham in Suffolk. He was made a Knight of the Garter in 1397 and so entered the most exclusive of the orders of chivalry. His marriage to Margaret, daughter of Premyslaus, Duke of Teschen, and maid of honour to Richard II's first queen, Anne of Bohemia, showed the regard in which he was held by the royal household. The Lancastrian coup of 1399 spelt disaster for Sir Simon, who was deprived of his lucrative keeperships and offices by the new king, Henry IV. His last ceremonial duty, the escorting of Richard's second queen, Isabel, into exile in 1400, was a melancholy assignment and although he retained his garter stall he seems never to have attended Chapters under the new regime. The death of his first wife in 1416 was the occasion for the making of one of the most splendid of English monumental brasses for Felbrigg church. Studded with the heraldry of Richard II and Bohemia, it was at once a defiant declaration and wistful symbol of the departed glory (see p.86).[2] When Sir Simon Felbrigg died in December 1442 and was buried with his second wife in the choir of the Norwich Blackfriars' church, his will provided for masses to be said for the soul of 'Richard, lately king of England' and instructed that Felbrigg be sold.

One of Sir Simon's trustees obtained the reversion of the estate and sold it in about 1450 to John Wymondham (later contracted to Wyndham), who had held land near Wymondham in south Norfolk since 1436. Wyndham took up residence in the face of angry demonstrations by the villagers. In 1461, the year of Lady Felbrigg's death, Sir John Felbrigg (the head of another branch of the family) and a band of sympathisers appeared at the house in Wyndham's absence and dragged his wife out of her locked room by the hair. Wyndham declared that he would be back by Michaelmas or there

The brass to Sir Simon Felbrigg and his first wife, Margaret (d.1416), in Felbrigg church; from an etching by J. S. Cotman

would be 'five hundred heads broke therefor', but eventually Sir John Felbrigg accepted a cash settlement and withdrew. Wyndham's son, another John, who succeeded in 1475, was, like Sir Edmund Bedingfeld of Oxburgh, knighted by Henry VII for service at the Battle of Stoke in 1487. He became, however, an associate of Edmund de la Pole, Earl of Suffolk, who in 1501 conspired with the Emperor Maximilian to overthrow the King. Sir John, closely implicated, died on the scaffold on 6 May 1502 alongside Tyrrel, prime suspect for the murder in 1483 of the Princes in the Tower, the young heirs to the Yorkist claim to the throne.

In spite of this setback, John's son Thomas made a name for himself in the navy, fighting against the French and ultimately gaining a place in Henry VIII's Council. He acquired great wealth, and may have built the earliest surviving parts of Felbrigg Hall. Under the south front are considerable remains of an early Tudor house: archways, a door with rich linenfold panelling, and, projecting under the forecourt, a cellar with a four-centred brick barrel vault. He died in 1522 and his son Edmund further bolstered the estate during the 1530s by acquiring Beeston Priory at a knockdown price during the Dissolution of the Monasteries. As High Sheriff of Norfolk Edmund organised the execution of the Ketts and their followers after the bloody suppression of their uprising in 1549.

With the inheritance of Edmund's son Roger in 1569, Felbrigg entered one of the most unhappy periods in its long history. The new squire set about the persecution of his neighbours and their connections with a zeal which, properly directed, might have consolidated his inheritance. He went to court at the least excuse, 'from stranded wrecks to straying houses and broken fences'.[3] His activities so depleted the resources of the estate that he was compelled to mortgage much of it to his wealthy cousin Sir John Wyndham, who presided over the flourishing junior branch of the family at Orchard Wyndham in Somerset. When Roger died in 1599, his only significant contribution to the distinction of the Norfolk branch was the institution of the modern spelling of Windham, and the widespread odium which then attached to the name. It fell to his youngest brother Thomas to receive this mixed inheritance, and providence gave him less than a year in which to make something of it.

NOTES

1 Edmund Bartell Junior, *Cromer Considered as a Watering Place*, 2nd ed., 1806, p.55.

2 J. Milner, 'Sir Simon Felbrigg, KG: The Lancastrian Revolution and Personal Fortune', *Norfolk Archaeology*, xxxvii, p.89.

3 R. W. Ketton-Cremer, *Felbrigg: The Story of a House*, 1962, p.26.

CHAPTER TWO
A NEW START

Thomas Windham began by renouncing everything that his brother had done and promised an immediate return to his father's more benign manorial customs. Moreover, as Roger had neglected to consult him, as an heir-at-law, over the mortgages to Sir John Wyndham, these were declared void. But Thomas made clear that, should he fail to marry and have children, then the reversion of the entire estate would pass to Sir John and with this important proviso:

Finally I do greatly desire that the said inheritance coming to my said cosin, the same might continually be inhabited, and the house of Felbrigg be dwelt upon, either by himself, or by some of his children of the name; so that the name might be continued with some countenance in this county, and in this lyneal succession, where the eldest house hath alwayes remained. Foreasmuch as otherwise if the lands should be alwayes in farm, and the rents continually be carryed out of the country, within a few years the name should there be utterly forgotten, hospitality abolished, and all come to ruine and desolation . . .[1]

As another Felbrigg winter settled in, Thomas Windham, having done more in a few months to enhance the family reputation than his brother had done in 30 years, died on 20 December 1599, leaving the hall in the occupation of his sister Jane Coningsby. She had kept house for him and was allowed to remain there until her death in 1608. For Sir John Wyndham it was a sensible and economic arrangement. After 1608 he had to run Felbrigg from Somerset, sending his servant John Blinman on arduous journeys across the country to draw up the accounts. One of Blinman's first jobs was to list the contents of the hall and the farm stock and to determine what should remain at Felbrigg; what should go to 'My Lord' at Orchard Wyndham; and what should be sent to 'Mr Thomas' in London. 'Mr Thomas', a London lawyer, was Sir John's

third son and the fact that he was now able to draw on the resources of the central part of the estate indicated that he had been chosen to refound the Norfolk Windhams.

Some of the best furnishings and plate were packed off to Orchard, including 'a Tester of a bed of Crimson velvet with vallance and curtains thereto belonging and curtains of Taffetie Sarsenett [silk taffeta]', together with 'two coverlettes, one of Arras and another of tapestrie'. Basic furniture, 'chairs, stools and suchlike' stayed at Felbrigg. The richest of Mrs Coningsby's clothes went to Orchard; some remained, while others were divided among her maids. The splendid plate, which would have been displayed at feasts in the old great hall (and which would no doubt have stood on the 'Arras Cupboard cloth' that went to Orchard), was split between Sir John and Thomas. A basin and cover in parcel gilt, a gilt standing cup, a 'great broad bowl' and a silver tankard, both with parcel gilt, and an engraved standing cup went to the father, while Mr Thomas got the spoons and a representative collection of grand pieces including a parcel gilt ewer and basin, a silver gilt goblet, a great silver bowl, and the remainder of the plate.[2]

In December 1620 Thomas married Elizabeth, daughter of Sir Rowland Lytton of Knebworth in Hertfordshire, and, in the expectation of founding a new dynasty at Felbrigg, he set about rebuilding the house with his father. The Chief Justice of the Common Pleas, Sir Henry Hobart, had assembled a considerable team of workmen for the rebuilding of Blickling Hall about eight miles south of Felbrigg in 1619.[3] The exact repetition of certain devices and details leaves no real doubt that Hobart's architect, Robert Lyminge, or a close associate, was also responsible for the new Felbrigg.

Work was already quite advanced when the sparse Felbrigg building accounts commence in

The south front, built by Sir John Wyndham and his son Thomas in 1621–4

1621.[4] Some of the earliest entries are in the hand of Elizabeth Windham, who was to die after giving birth to an heir in 1622. In February Matthews the bricklayer was paid for paving the cellars. He was also responsible for a number of brick windows (probably mullioned and rendered to look like stone, as in the 1624 wings at Blickling). Edward Stanyon the plasterer, whose splendid ceilings may be seen at Blickling, also received payment. It was quite usual at this period for the builder of a house to enter into separate agreements with numerous contractors, so we find mention of several other craftsmen: Stockdale the carpenter and 'his bargin for the stairs' of £33; Christopher the joiner, Linacre the glazier, and in 1624 Smith the mason, who was paid for the two stone lions which surmount the east and west gables, and no doubt made the other parapet figures. The house must have

been nearly complete at this time, and there is some evidence to suggest that there was more to it than the south front we see today. The accounts indicate that parts of the ancient house were retained. In February 1623 'the hard stone men' were paid 2s 6d 'For setting the harth pase [stone] in the ould great chamber', which must have been part of an existing structure and probably outside the present 1620s work.[5] In the plan drawn up by William Samwell for William Windham I in the early 1670s, the walls were hatched in two different tones to distinguish new work from existing walls retained. This clearly shows a large rectangular projection to the north of the present Great Hall which could easily have accommodated Stockdale's new staircase and other rooms.

The design of Jacobean Felbrigg was typical of its period. The ground plan with the central porch leading into a screens passage with the great hall to the west and the butteries, pantry and kitchen to the east finds more than one parallel in the plans of

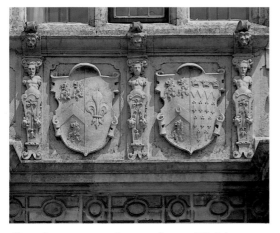

Above the entrance are the coats of arms of Sir John Wyndham of Orchard Wyndham in Somerset, his wife Joan Portman, their son Thomas and his first wife Elizabeth Lytton. They celebrated the re-establishment of the family at Felbrigg by building the south front

houses drawn by the Smythsons in the late sixteenth century. But it bears a particularly intimate resemblance to Crewe Hall in Cheshire, which was begun in 1615 by Sir Randulph Crewe, an ambitious lawyer who was to become Lord Chief Justice in 1625. He had Norfolk connections and would have been well known to Sir Henry Hobart and Thomas Windham, who were both also lawyers. The south front of Crewe has the same arrangement of bays, a similar rectangular central porch and the same group of three chimneystacks rising behind the roof.[6]

The significance of the house as a new start for the Windhams in Norfolk is proclaimed in its decoration. The coats of arms above the front door are those of Sir John Wyndham and of his son Thomas and their wives. The involvement of two generations is also implied in the heraldic decoration at Blickling, but where Felbrigg differs from most houses of the period is in the prominence given to the great religious message of its first-floor parapet, 'GLORIA DEO IN EXCELSIS'. Comparable openwork inscriptions are found at Castle Ashby, Northamptonshire (built in 1624) and at Temple Newsam in Yorkshire (c.1630, renewed in metal, 1788). It would certainly have appealed to the Jacobean taste for the witty 'device' to place 'Glory to God in the High-

est' on the highest part of the building, but Thomas Windham was perhaps mindful of those powerful passages in Deuteronomy where the Law is given in the context of establishing a place in a new land: 'What man is there that hath built a new house, and hath not dedicated it?' (xx.5). Included among the misfortunes predicted for those who forget God in Chapter 28 is '... thou shalt build a house and not dwell therein; thou shalt plant a vineyard and not use the fruit thereof'. It was a very real prospect. Elizabeth Windham had already gone and soon Sir Henry Hobart was to die before he had a chance to enjoy Blickling, but Thomas Windham and his father both lived on for many years and the branch which had been replanted in Norfolk flourished anew.

NOTES

1 Quoted in full in *Felbrigg*, p.28.

2 Norfolk and Norwich Record Office (NNRO), MF 122.

3 See C. Stanley-Millson and J. Newman, 'Blickling Hall: The Building of a Jacobean Mansion', *Architectural History*, xxix, 1986, pp.1–43.

4 NNRO, MF 122.

5 A point made by John Phibbs, *Felbrigg Park: A Survey of the Landscape*, 1982, p.17, n.15. For Stanyon's work, see also the *Plasterers' Company Quarterage*, detailing payments to him in December 1621 and in May 1622 and 1623, quoted in Clare Gapper, *Decorative Plasterwork Ceilings in London, 1540–1640*, MA Report, University of London, 1990.

6 See P. de Figueiredo and J. Treuherz, *Cheshire Country Houses*, 1988, pp.66–71. Crewe Hall was much altered by E. M. Barry after a fire in 1866, but the south front is still recognisable and its original appearance is recorded in a painting of c.1710. I am grateful to Andor Gomme for suggesting Crewe as a work of Robert Lyminge.

FAMILY TREE

Owners of Felbrigg are shown in CAPITALS

Asterisk denotes portrait in the house

JOHN WYNDHAM = Margaret Clifton
(d.1475)

Sir JOHN WYNDHAM = Margaret Howard
(d.1502)

Sir THOMAS WYNDHAM = Eleanor Scrope
(d.1522)

Sir EDMUND WYNDHAM = Susan Townsend
(d.1569)

Sir John Wyndham = Elizabeth Sydenham
of Orchard Wyndham
(d.1574)

ROGER WINDHAM = Mary Heydon
(d.1599)

Judge Francis Windham* = Elizabeth Bacon
(d.1592)

THOMAS WINDHAM
(d.1599)

Jane
(d.1608)

John Wyndham = Florence Wadham
(d.1572)

Sir John Wyndham = Joan Portman
(1558–1645)

John Wyndham = Katherine Hopton
(d.1642)

(1) Elizabeth Lytton (d.1622) m.1620 = THOMAS WINDHAM (1585–1654) = (2) Elizabeth Mede m.c.1644

Sir Joseph Ashe, Bt* (1617/18–86) = Mary Wilson* (c.1632–1705)

Sir George Wyndham = Frances Davy
of Cromer
(d.1663)

Wyndhams of Orchard Wyndham and Petworth

JOHN WINDHAM (1622–65) = (1) Jane Godfrey (d.1652) (2) Jane Townshend (d.1656) (3) Dorothy Ogle (d.1664) (4) Lady Frances Annesley

WILLIAM WINDHAM I* (1647–89) = Katherine* (1652–1729) m.1669

Mary* (1653–85) = Horatio 1st Viscount Townshend* of Raynham (1630–87) m.1673

Francis Wyndham = Sarah Dayrell
(1656–1730)

ASHE WINDHAM* (1673–1749) m.1709 = Elizabeth Dobyns* (1693–1736)

Col. William Windham* (1674–1730) of Earsham = Anne Tyrrell m.1705

Joseph Windham (1683–1746) = Martha Ashe m.1715

James Windham (1687–1724)

Thomas Wyndham (1686–1752) = Anne Edwin

WILLIAM WINDHAM II* (1717–61) m.1750 = (2) Sarah Hicks* (1710–92) (1) = Robert Lukin

Charles* (d.1747)

John (1709–80) = Mary (1717–89) m.1734

John Wyndham (1732–65) = Elizabeth Dalton

WILLIAM WINDHAM III* (1750–1810) = Cecilia Forrest (1750–1824) m.1798

Rev. George William Lukin later Dean of Wells (1739–1812) = Catherine Doughty

Joseph* (1739–1810) of Earsham

George Wyndham* (1762–1810) = Marianne Bacon

Vice-Admiral WILLIAM LUKIN* (1768–1833) assumed name of WINDHAM 1824 = Anne Thellusson* (1775–1849)

Robert*   George*   John*

WILLIAM HOWE WINDHAM* (1802–54) = Lady Sophia Hervey* (1811–63) m.1835

Cecilia Ann Windham* (1803–74) = Henry Baring

Major-Gen. Charles Ashe Windham* (1810–70)

Maria Augusta Windham* (1805–71) m.1826 = (1) George Thomas Wyndham* (1806–30) m.1826 (2) William, Viscount Ennismore, later 2nd Earl of Listowel (1801–56) m.1831

Marianne Charlotte Wyndham (1804–42) = Rev. Cremer Cremer (1795–1867) m.1829

WILLIAM FREDERICK WINDHAM* (1840–66) = Anne Agnes Rogers (alias Willoughby)

JOHN KETTON* (1808–72) bought Felbrigg 1863 = Rachel Anne Blake (d.1885)

Frederick Howe Lindsey Bacon Windham (1864–96) = Katherine Eveleigh Batt

John

ROBERT WILLIAM KETTON (1854–1935)

Marion (d.1898)

Gertrude (d.1895)

Rachel Anna* (1841–1932) = Thomas Wyndham Cremer (1834–94)

WYNDHAM CREMER CREMER* (1870–1933) added name of KETTON 1924 = Emily Bayly* (1882–1952) m.1905

ROBERT WYNDHAM KETTON-CREMER* (1906–69)   Richard Thomas Wyndham Ketton-Cremer (1909–41)

CHAPTER THREE
WILLIAM AND KATHERINE WINDHAM

With the coming of the Civil War in 1642, Thomas Windham became an active supporter of Parliament. As High Sheriff of Norfolk in 1639–40 it had been his task to collect the King's hated 'Ship Money' tax from the county. Most of Norfolk became solidly Parliamentarian and Thomas served on the Committee for the Eastern Association. His elder son John became a captain of horse. Whereas the few Royalist houses, for example Oxburgh, that found themselves behind enemy lines suffered some violence, for Felbrigg the war meant only anxiety and economic hardship.

Thomas Windham died on 1 March 1654, attended by Dr Thomas Browne, the author of *Religio Medici*, one of the most famous seventeenth-century confessions of faith. The eleven-year reign at Felbrigg of his son John was uneventful so far as the house and estate were concerned but was marked by personal tragedies. He buried three wives, produced no surviving heir and died in 1665 little more than a year after his fourth marriage. His half-brother William, who had been born to Thomas Windham's second wife, Elizabeth Mede, in 1647, came of age in 1668 and during the next 21 years was to leave an indelible mark on Felbrigg. In 1669 he married Katherine, daughter of Sir Joseph Ashe, a wealthy merchant of Twickenham in Middlesex who traded with the Low Countries. Both William and Katherine made conscientious records of estate and household management and are depicted with considerable panache in two portraits in the Dining Room. Katherine, who survived her husband by 40 years, became a most likeable matriarch and was the backbone of the family until her death in 1729.

William Windham ran the estate himself, recording all his doings in two vellum-covered ledgers.[1] The second of these, stained a bright green with brass clasps, is among the most important records of estate management in England at this period. An early entry of 1670 contains one of the first references to the garden: 'To Collins one old Oake when I Inlarged the Parlour Garden at Felbrigg'. This note also sheds light on the Jacobean house, confirming that the Parlour was either in or near the rectangular structure mentioned earlier, north of the Great Hall. Some indication of the size of the house at this time is conveyed by another note, presumably connected with hearth tax: 'There are 14 Chimneys in the House'. And there are numerous references to tree planting, which was William Windham's great joy (see p.89).

The prospect of major building operations was heralded in 1675, when he noted, 'I felled all the Timber used about my new building at Felbrigg'. But the Green Book does not give the whole story, as Windham was evidently reluctant to make a neat account of still incomplete building work, which, as it turned out, was to continue beyond his death. We must rely also on the less explicit rough notes in his earlier ledger.

Drawings for the extension of the house were prepared for Windham by the gentleman architect William Samwell in August 1674. The first ground plan proposed to double its size with three new fronts around a courtyard. The second, in February 1675, reduced the scheme by half to a new west wing and, on the north-east corner, a one-room-deep addition to the back of the main Jacobean pile. 'I persuaded Mr Samwell to draw this against his fancye', Windham notes on the second drawing, 'by reason I thought his first design too bigg & not convenient, which caused him to write . . . [and here in Samwell's own hand] "This ill fourmed Beare",' after which Windham resumes, 'I like this very well altering y^e Closet & Staires.' Below his signature are the words 'built Anno: 75'. The handsome drawing of the west elevation by Samwell

William Windham I (1647–89), who built the west front; by Sir Peter Lely (Dining Room)

shows yet another phase in the design process. Whereas the first two had suggested a west façade which included and remodelled the west gable of the Jacobean house, the elevation drawing expresses the wing as a distinct unit, and implies the arresting contrast between old and new which the west front presents today.

William Samwell already had to his credit the King's House at Newmarket in Cambridgeshire (1668–71), The Grange at Northington, Hampshire (c.1670), and a major part of Ham House in Surrey (1672–4). He was a skilled practitioner of the new Restoration classicism and his front at Felbrigg preserves better than any surviving example of his work his sophisticated grasp of detail and proportion.

But Samwell died in the summer of 1676. Given that the exterior of the west wing was not finished until about 1686, it is unlikely that he saw more than the building of the north-eastern extension. This has a different string course from the west wing and it is on this part of the second drawing

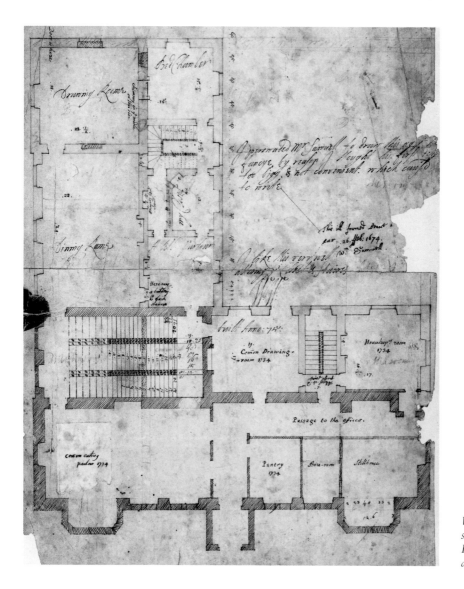

William Samwell's second plan, of February 1675, for a new west wing

Samwell's elevation drawing for the west front, c.1675

that Windham's words 'built Anno: 75' are in-scribed. Indeed the west wing itself could not conveniently have been built unless this part had gone up first. For it contains a handsome new stair-case which would have been essential to the family if, as seems likely, the great new stairs proposed for the west wing by Samwell destroyed the Jacobean ones. So the timber felled in 1675 was probably for this first phase of work.

From at least 1681 Windham had been engaged in other building projects which included a new brew-house. With the demise of Samwell we have to speculate as to who could have directed the substantial works of the 1680s. The brew-house accounts introduce three important contractors: Skidmore the master carpenter, his assistant Thomas Vidler, and Skerry the bricklayer.[2] Skid-more was to disappear from the scene quite quickly but he was the author of an unexecuted plan for a new free-standing service building which incor-porated some of the functions from the rejected parts of Samwell's ambitious first plan: bakehouse, meat room, dairy, pump-house, wash-house and scullery.

On the other side of the drawing is a plan for the cellars beneath the west wing. So perhaps it may

have been Skidmore who carried Samwell's plans forward in the first instance. His assistant Vidler was to stay on until the next century and received extensive payments. Miles Skerry, variously des-cribed as bricklayer and mason, may have been responsible for the wonderful brickwork of the new wing, and there are also payments to a Michael Skerry. Especially interesting in view of Samwell's house for Charles II at Newmarket is the note in August 1683 that a 'Newmarket man' was paid 'to set the clamp of 100,000 bricks'. These were prob-ably special bricks for the facing of the wing, and in September Vidler was recompensed for paying another brickmaker, Spink, for 166,100 bricks and tiles.[3] In 1685 Windham ordered the felling of more timber 'used about my building'.[4] Sir Jacob Astley of Melton Constable, whose great new house was rising at the same time, provided some lead for Felbrigg. Wortlie the plumber was paid at Rayn-ham, another important Norfolk house and the home of Katherine's sister, Lady Townshend.[5]

We cannot ascribe all of these payments to the west wing with certainty because of the other projects running alongside it, notably the repair and extension of the park wall (see p.92) and the con-struction of new stables. By 1686, however, the

The plaster ceiling of the Great Parlour (now Drawing Room), dated 1687, is probably by Edward Goudge

date on one of the west front rainwater heads, the main structure was complete. On the ground floor the new wing provided a great staircase, a new Great Parlour for dining, and beyond it a smaller withdrawing-room. On the first floor were two large rooms and a pair of closets. There was much fitting out to do. The marvellous plaster ceiling of the Great Parlour (now the Drawing Room) is dated 1687, and is clearly by the plasterer who made the contemporary ceilings at Melton Constable – probably Edward Goudge, one of the greatest craftsmen of the period. In May 1688 there is an early payment to Cornwell the painter, and Goodwife Hilton was sent in to clean the building.[6] In April the following year panels for the Great Parlour were supplied by Knowles the joiner from Holt,[7] who was paid that September for laying floors in 'the New Building'.[8] In May Caston the local carpenter (possibly a member of the Cawston family who were to work as estate carpenters until the late nineteenth century) was paid for framing the cellar windows on the garden side and for laying the floor of the great stairs.[9] The final touches were being made to the Great Parlour in October when 1s was paid for 'a seale skin to Rub the wainscot', 2s 'for lyne to hang the picktures in the new parlour'.[10] Cornwell varnished the panels from a scaffold made by Caston.[11] A few later payments are recorded: a certain Hewit for marble, presumably in connection with fireplaces (such as that now in the Library) and a stone cutter for the two pine

cones which sat at either end of the roof ridge until the 1750s (see p.39).

The west wing caused a revolution in the local architecture. Aylsham Old Hall was being built simultaneously and not far away by another branch of the family and exhibits many identical details, as do numerous houses and imposing barns in Aylsham, Coltishall and other parts of the Bure valley until the mid-eighteenth century. But not everyone was so impressed by the amenities of the 'New Appartment'. Roger North, the virtuoso who lived at Rougham in Norfolk, while acknowledging the general acclaim, was particularly critical of the staircase which the local carpenters had built in what is now the Dining Room to a plan different from the one envisaged by Samwell. North wrote of it: 'however pompous and costly in the frame and finishing, doth not stupifie the sense, so as to make the pains of mounting three or four stretching flights insensible.'[12]

The last payments for the exterior of the new wing are recorded by Katherine Windham as executrix of her husband's will, for, as she wrote in her first little notebook, 'My Dear Dear Husband left me the 9th June 1689 having made me Hapy 20 years.'[13] William Windham's life at Felbrigg had been a reasonably tranquil one, after some initial quarrels with importunate relations, and in spite of the persistant entreaties of Sir John Hobart of Blickling, he had managed to avoid much involvement in politics: 'I confess I take soe much delight in my Nursery and Garden that I don't envye the Knight the honour of being in the house', he had written in 1679.[14]

A small plan shows the house and garden in August 1691 (see p.83), more or less as Windham must have left it. The house has now assumed its present shape and facing the west wing is the Parlour Garden divided from the Flower Garden by a terrace. In front of the house itself is the little court, then two parallel walls with gateways leading to the large open coach-yard. From an eighteenth-century plan of the same area (see p.21) we can identify the group of buildings to the west of the coach-yard as a barn, coach-house, stable, coachman's stable and garden house. East of the yard is a narrow rectangular stable block and to the east of this the orchard and a square dove-house. Running at right-angles to the new west wing and defining a partial courtyard north of the house are two substantial ranges of service buildings.

Katherine Windham presided over Felbrigg and its family during the minority of her eldest son, Ashe, who had been given her maiden name. He was now eighteen and, after Eton, was completing his education at its sister foundation, King's College, Cambridge. Katherine Windham's love for Felbrigg and her children shines out of the numerous letters and accounts that record her life. She had been a girl of seventeen when she came to Felbrigg and the earliest entries in her notebook, some of them in French, record fashionable clothes and trimmings, caged birds and a book on how to care for them, perfume, money lost and won at cards, gifts to the poor and books.[15] Most of the latter were devotional but a significant number were medical and herbal, and later she was relied upon by the family for herbal remedies.

Katherine Windham (1652–1729), who ran the Felbrigg estate in her widowhood; by Sir Peter Lely and Studio (Dining Room)

There was much to occupy her bereavement. Her management of the estate and of the family finances is recorded in her *Fair Accounts since Midsummer 1689*.[16] The family vault was repaired and a monument commemorating her husband ordered for the church from Grinling Gibbons. In 1687–8 she hung her drawing-room with crimson and green damask with green and white fringing for £64. A large inlaid table and hanging looking-glass with a pair of candlestands were £18. She bought ten elbow chairs for £6 15s from Thomas Arne (a Covent Garden upholsterer and the father of the composer), had them japanned for £2 15s, upholstered for £4 4s, and everyday case covers made for £3. Eight silver sconces were £42, and for the fireplace she bought silver andirons in three pieces, which, with matching dogs, shovel and tongs with silver knobs, came to £44. She also had four cane chairs with cushions (there are three such chairs beneath the stairs and the remains of a third in the Lower Turnery, see p.80) and two dutch chairs.

Her *Book of Cookery and Housekeeping*, begun in 1707, is a fascinating record of a wealthy family's diet at the period.[17] 'Artificial Sturgion', made from a whole boiled calf's head from which the bones are removed, sounds unappetising but there are many recipes that would be popular today. Some are named after family and friends: 'Lord Townshend's Puding', 'my son's Rice Puding', 'a very good Carroway Cake My Sister Townshend' and so on. There are remedies for getting flies out of rooms and the section 'Concerning Buggs' recommends smearing the bedding with broken-up cucumbers or covering one's face and neck with lemon juice and wormwood.

NOTES

1 NNRO, WKC 5/151–52.
2 Eg WKC 5/151 p.188.
3 Ibid. p.226.
4 NNRO, WKC 5/152 p.198.
5 NNRO, WKC 5/151 p.226.
6 NNRO, WKC 5/162.
7 NNRO, WKC 5/160.
8 NNRO, WKC 5/162.
9 NNRO, WKC 5/166.
10 NNRO, WKC 5/163.
11 NNRO, WKC 5/164.
12 BM Add. MS 32540.
13 NNRO, WKC 6/12.
14 *Felbrigg*, p.68.
15 NNRO, WKC 6/14.
16 NNRO, WKC 6/16.
17 NNRO, WKC 6/457.

CHAPTER FOUR

THE EIGHTEENTH CENTURY

In 1692 Patrick St Clair was appointed as Ashe's tutor and in 1693, the year before the new squire came of age, the two of them set off on the Grand Tour. On their return in 1696 St Clair was presented to the living of Aylmerton. In 1694 we find the first recorded payment towards a major new building. It is listed in Katherine Windham's personal account amongst other payments: 'Deals Green House £9 4s',[1] a figure repeated in 1708 in her memorandum of the costs of building the Orangery, which was one of the major undertakings of Ashe's early years. That it was projected so early is confirmed by the rough pencilled outline of the building which was added to the plan of 1691 mentioned earlier, and in 1697 the young orange trees were bought for £21.[2]

'I design to find sashes workmanship shutters doors pavement for the orenge house', Katherine wrote in one of her typically chatty letters of February 1705, 'and you to find Bricke, lime, Timber, Tile & Cariage but all the money must be deducted out of what you owe me, which is at least 350, for I cant supply my children on your account & find money for everything. Wish I could & it should be at your service.' In the same letter she makes clear that there was still work to do in the west wing and suggests that Ashe 'may let alone the Glasse & Harths & Chairs till another time for with the bed curtains & Ha[n]gings the romes may be used this year the smell of the paint will not be quickly out'[3]; an aside probably connected with a small group of drawings for two of the first-floor rooms (the present Rose and Red Bedrooms) in the west wing, made to calculate the size of hangings and to indicate different treatments for fireplaces and chimney-glasses. In November 1704 Elden the carpenter had been paid for work about the new building.[4] Whereas the windows of the Great Parlour had iron bars[5] and must, therefore, have been of the old

mullion-and-transom type with leaded lights, as shown in Samwell's drawing, these two rooms are shown with sashes, and this novel type of window was to be the most prominent feature of the new Orangery.

The drawings for the Orangery are unsigned, but Ashe may have been its architect. A plain but well-proportioned building, it is a perfect neighbour for the west wing, and might have been more decorative had Katherine Windham not been in charge of operations in Ashe's absence, for the letter quoted above includes the remark, 'We country folks are too dull to understand what you mean by ornaments.'

Mathematical instruments had been bought for Ashe in 1690/1 and there is a contemporary payment to 'Gibson designing master'.[6] This was the year of the little plan of Felbrigg and its gardens which may indeed have been one of Ashe's early efforts at surveying. For the Orangery he would, however, have needed the assistance of a very competent builder. His mother's account lists the workmen.[7] The bricklayer, Edge, was probably one of the family of masons which had been associated with the Townshends at nearby Raynham since the early seventeenth century and was no doubt recommended to Katherine by her sister, Lady Townshend. The only ornamental feature of Edge's beautiful brickwork was the carefully cut roll moulding which defines the corners of the window embrasures; these were special bricks formed by Boleken 'Brick cuter'. Vidler the carpenter was still at Felbrigg and worked alongside another man, Burows, who was probably the Aylsham carpenter who did so much at Blickling around this time.[8] Knowles the joiner from Holt figures once more with a colleague, Hopson, who was paid £92, a vast sum compared with the others, which may represent the sash windows, glazed by Briggins for just

Ashe Windham (1673–1749); by Sir Godfrey Kneller (Dining Room)

The Orangery, built by Ashe Windham by 1707

over £24. The shutters were made by a Mr Morris. In August 1707 Katherine wrote that 'the Orange House pavement goes on well & looks fine'[9] and in December that year Mr Singleton – probably the mason and sculptor Robert Singleton of Bury St Edmunds – was paid £102 for stonework which could have included the Orangery floor and the fine carved sills as well perhaps as paving in the garden.[10] In this instance he may only have been the supplier, because Robert Rush the Norwich stone-cutter was also paid £13 in February 1708.

One of the notable features of the estate accounts during the first decade of the eighteenth century is the crescendo of activity in the brickworks. William Barrett received advance payment in December 1702 for 100,000 bricks to be made in the coming year. In November 1703 200,000 more were ordered and the same amount in October

1704.[11] This intense period of activity during which the kiln was fed with bracken, rushes, brushwood and whatever happened to be harvested at the time, subsided towards the end of the decade. The Orangery was one cause and so was the continuing repair of the park wall, and there was work on other estate buildings. But Ashe had also taken on the task of completely rebuilding the domestic offices at the house around a spacious courtyard and remodelling the garden. These changes are recorded in a plan which was probably drawn in the 1740s and which shows that an attempt had been made to simplify and open up the surroundings of the house (see p.21).

Annotated drawings in Ashe's hand show how deeply involved he was in surveying the site of the new service buildings on the west side of the house and overcoming the problems of differential levels which it presented. The west side of the new court-yard contained servants' hall, kitchen, bakehouse and meat room. The north range accommodated a deer house or dairy, the wash-house, malt-house and brew-house, and a new granary ran at right-angles on the east side. The south side was formed by a narrow building which contained scullery, pastry room, dry larder, the cook's chamber and, at the far end, the keeper's chamber. Most of these buildings survive, and were probably complete by 1711, when a joiner was paid for some of the wash-house furniture,[12] but the south range was to be replaced by Ashe's son in the 1750s and the north and west ranges were substantially remodelled thereafter. Only the granary perfectly preserves its original character and is one of the most pleasing buildings on the estate.

Money was not a problem for Ashe Windham, whose father's various loans and investments produced a healthy income. These new buildings of course implied a large household. His liveried servants wore blue coats with red waistcoats and included Dutch and Italian footmen. The park keeper was allowed the distinction of a 'coat and waistcoat of Green Cloth and breeches of green shagg'. Between 1695 and 1709 Ashe spent nearly £243 on his own clothes and £187 on livery.[13] He was in every respect an eligible young man and the

decade which saw so much building activity at Felbrigg witnessed much else in the life of the family. In 1704 his younger brother, William, lost his leg at Blenheim and wrote home to his mother about it with extraordinary courage and cheerfulness. Ashe was elected to Parliament in 1708, but gave up the seat two years later. Early in 1708 he met the love of his life in Hester Buckworth and showered her with over £285 worth of jewels, much to his mother's annoyance.[14] In anticipation of their marriage, Katherine decided to decamp to a house of her own at Braxted in Essex; her accounts at this period record extensive payments to different upholsterers and cabinetmakers. But Hester Buckworth died of smallpox before the year was out. The large portrait of her, which hangs above the door to the Dining Room in the Stair Hall, must have acquired added poignancy as the years went by, especially when Ashe's relationship with the attractive but neurotic Elizabeth Dobyns – married on the rebound in 1709 with another £472 worth of jewels – gradually went sour. Their only child, William, was born in 1717 and three years later the squire and his wife finally separated. The 1720s were difficult years in which the family lost huge sums in the collapse of the South Sea

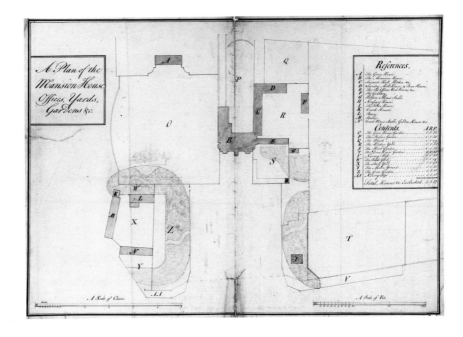

This plan, probably of the 1740s, shows Ashe Windham's Orangery (A) and the domestic offices (C, D, E, F, G), which he rebuilt around a spacious courtyard (R)

Hester Buckworth, Ashe Windham's fiancée, who died of smallpox in 1708, before they could marry; Studio of Sir Godfrey Kneller (Stair Hall)

Bubble and in which Ashe contracted a mysterious and chronic illness that was to keep him away from Felbrigg for long periods. These absences were much regretted by friends and neighbours but Patrick St Clair, who was left in charge, wrote a series of letters between 1729 and 1741 which paint a vivid and detailed picture of life in this corner of Norfolk and were published by Wyndham Ketton-Cremer in *Country Neighbourhood*.

When Katherine Windham died in 1729 at the age of 78, Ashe's own generation was already falling away. His brother James had died at sea near Honduras in 1724. Colonel William Windham died in 1730 and Ashe's estranged wife Elizabeth followed in 1736. Many hopes must have been pinned on the next generation, represented by the solitary figure of Ashe's son William.

William Windham II was destined by upbringing and temperament to form as strong a bond with Felbrigg as any of its previous inhabitants. He was saved from the rigours of boarding school and did not attend any university. Patrick St Clair remained at Felbrigg to instruct him, and in 1723 Benjamin Stillingfleet was appointed his personal tutor. This eccentric and agreeable scholar, the grandson of the

Bishop of Worcester, was to publish works on mathematics, music, society and natural history. The blue worsted stockings which he wore at the literary soirées held by Mrs Vesey became a shorthand for intellectual womankind. If one looks at the books which his pupil bought for the library at Felbrigg, it is not difficult to see how influential Stillingfleet had been in forming the very catholic tastes of the new squire, whose coming of age was marked in 1737 by one of Stillingfleet's lengthy poems, 'An Essay on Conversation', which began:

> WINDHAM with Diligence awhile attend,
> Nor scorn the Instructions of an older Friend.[16]

In 1738 tutor and pupil set out on a tour of the Continent from which they were not to return until 1742. They went first to Geneva and then spent some months in Rome. But by the winter of 1739–40 they were back in Geneva. Here with a group of young English friends and their tutors Windham formed a club known as 'the Common Room'. Their light-hearted but historic expedition in June 1741 to the Mer de Glace is still commemorated by a plaque on the edge of the glacier. In the plays which they put on for their own amusement Stillingfleet wrote the music and was in charge of the stage machinery. Windham's extravagant behaviour was later fondly recollected by another member of the Common Room, Richard Aldworth:

Windham, tall, thin, and narrow-chested, would vie with Price in every feat of strength and agility, and so far he succeeded that he was known through London by the name of *Boxing Windham*; whilst few knew his quiet friend Mr Price could box at all. Fewer yet could divine that Mr Windham would have excelled in almost every pursuit but those he was seen to follow; that he possessed Greek, Latin, Spanish, and French, to a high degree; and knew something of Dutch and German. This was, however, the fact; and from those various sources, his amazing parts, equally quick and retentive, had drawn and amassed treasures of science and amusement, which was the more striking from his apparent dissipation: he was besides a mathematician, mechanic and draughtsman; could and did build vessels, and navigate them himself; in short, he was every thing.

He had an utter abhorrence of restraint, which made him love to associate with those that put him under none at all: here he might throw his legs against the chimney, round himself into a hoop in his elbow chair, and at the same time read one subject, and converse on another. . .[17]

The lack of restraint was to get him into trouble. In 1740 Windham was betrothed to Elisabeth de Chapeaurouge, the daughter of the First Syndic of Geneva, but his image of her was to fade rapidly on his return to England, although it was not until 1751 that he finally extricated himself from this commitment, at some considerable expense. Windham and Stillingfleet began their return journey via the Low Countries in July 1742. In the seven years before his father's death, William was to pursue his own existence away from Felbrigg, taking a house in London with his friend Robert Price of Foxley and renting country retreats in Essex and Warwickshire. He developed a long-lasting friendship with David Garrick which is commemorated in a charming double portrait by Francis Hayman that Garrick commissioned in about 1745.

In the early 1740s Hayman had collaborated with the architect James Paine on a number of jobs in the north of England and it was probably through this connection that Windham came to employ Paine at Felbrigg. There is a suggestion that someone else was also considered but we do not know who it was. A drawing for the Cabinet bay window was made by a 'Mr Dagnia', whose portrait was to occupy a central position in William Windham II's redecorated Great Parlour (see p.65). There is also a group of mid-eighteenth-century survey plans of the house and grounds which are possibly of the 1740s and not obviously the work of Paine. But these are the only clues we have and it is evident that by 1749 work had begun at Felbrigg under Paine's direction. From then on we can follow its progress through Windham's account books and in the numerous friendly and animated letters of instruction which he sent to his agent Robert Frary. Frary also worked for Windham's neighbour Mr Doughty of Hanworth, who was often used as a sounding board for the squire's architectural ideas. Windham's letters are packed with miscellaneous

requests and include much discourse on horses and lengthy descriptions of excitements in the hunting field.

The first task for Paine was the construction of a new service wing to take the place of the narrow southern service range put up by Ashe, as well as some alterations to the north range. This new wing was important to Windham not just because it allowed for the creation of a new servants' hall, steward's room and audit room but because it also incorporated the workshops where he could follow the many practical interests hinted at by Richard Aldworth, which included wood-turning and bookbinding (see p.80). Fireworks had been a

William Windham II (1717–61) wearing Hussar uniform, which he may have acquired during his Continental tour in 1738–42; attributed to James Dagnia (Stair Hall)

James Paine's original design for the new Stair Hall (re-arranged to show the four walls in one plane). The medals proposed for the north wall were replaced by a further pair of niches and busts

passion of his for some years and he reminded Frary to keep a fire in the shop where they were stored so that the powder did not become damp.[18] After Frary's death in 1753, his successor Robert Thurston evidently continued this practice until the great explosion of 27 December 1755, which probably brought Windham's interest in pyrotechnics to a premature end. It entirely destroyed the firework shop, whose roof was blown over the top of the granary and was later found blazing in the coalyard. Windows were smashed throughout the service yard and everyone considerably shaken up.[19]

The new service wing also provided useful storage space in the early 1750s, when the state rooms were in turmoil. The wing's foundations had been dug by July 1749 and on 13 August John Baxter was paid for carting 20,000 bricks to the 'Offices'. The builder was Francis Pank and in November of the same year he was paid for making floors and ceilings. In November rubbish was being cleared out of the new building and just before Christmas a neighbour, Bozoon Brigge, who must have had pale brick earth not available at Felbrigg, was paid

for the white paving bricks of the workshop floors.[20] It is in the construction of these attractive service rooms that we first encounter the joiner George Church, who was to make nearly all the fitted woodwork and some of the movable furniture during the five years of Windham's extensive remodelling.

The servants' wing was being furnished in January 1751 and by now much progress had been made in the house. The 1680s west wing was deepened on its east side by an extension that housed ground- and first-floor passages (the present Stone and West Corridors), bringing greater privacy to rooms which had previously opened into one another. At the north end a two-storey polygonal bay extended what had been the Drawing Room and the two little rooms above it. As the work became ever more complex there was a need for someone to be placed in overall control of the site. Frary suggested Church, but Windham was doubtful and consulted Paine, who in May sent Mr Hull, an experienced builder who had already worked for him in Yorkshire and whose only drawback was the habit of 'getting Loose for a day or two', which he had 'promised to reform'.[21]

The old Drawing Room with its new bay window was now to be known as the Cabinet, and the accounts sometimes refer to it as the 'best room'.

Although tackled first, the Cabinet was clearly conceived as the climax of a sequence of ground-floor rooms. The Great Parlour was also re-modelled with handsome new joinery, and the Eating Room (now the Dining Room) took the place of the 1680s staircase, whose successor rose immediately to the east. On the first floor the removal of the old stairs and the introduction of the bay made possible a suite of two bedrooms with spacious and richly appointed dressing-rooms (see p.74), and with the luxury of a decent corridor. This left a little gap at the south end and here Windham contrived his own modest dressing-room (now known as the Grey Dressing Room). It did not need to be large because it had a private door into the great new Library which took up nearly half of the south front and which communicated with the bedroom (now the Book Room) which he shared with his wife.

Sarah Lukin (née Hicks) was the widow of Robert Lukin of Dunmow in Essex, by whom she had had three children. When, at the age of 40, Sarah married Windham in February 1750, the two had been living together for several years and she was already heavily pregnant with his child. In May she gave birth to a son, another William and, like his father, an only child. It was after this that Windham began the complex and expensive negotiations

that would release him from his obligations to Elizabeth de Chapeaurouge in Geneva.[22]

The work at Felbrigg was subject to the usual delays, and Windham became irate. On 3 March 1752 he wrote:

I have just received a letter from Paine with a drawing of the staircase which I send you. He says he has had an inflammation of his eyes which has prevented his finishing the drawings &c humbug. I have wrote to Mr Field to speak to him roundly & told him we would send him heads of accusations from Felbrigg. I think the staircase too much ornamented according to that draught.[23]

Especially stressful was the business of coordinating the London craftsmen to produce their goods in time to be shipped by Mr Worsted to Felbrigg in June:

Worsted is come and I have been in the cursedest passion imaginable with all the workmen about the things. Carter who was to have done the chimney-piece sent me word that he could not get the chimney done before the end of next month upon which I sent to stop all his doings & sure I would not have the chimney at all . . . as for Biggs I have stopped all his work & will send you the drawings for to have the chimney for the eating parlour to be done by our own workmen. Bladwell will have everything ready by Thursday & we will endeavour to keep Worsted till the medals [see p.63] are ready and will be sent down. The pictures are now preparing and will be ready very soon . . .[24]

Bladwell the upholsterer, of Bow Street, Covent Garden, who also provided furniture for Uppark in Sussex and Holkham in Norfolk, proved to be the most reliable of the London men and was paid very large sums for furniture of superb quality, including some lovely Rococo looking-glasses in the Cabinet. Mirror glass was still extraordinarily expensive and Windham obtained measured drawings of all the seventeenth-century mirrors in the house so that the new frames would fit their plates.[25] The gilded picture frames which do so much to enliven the rooms were made by either René Duffour in Soho or Thomas Quintin, who worked on site at Felbrigg. Quintin[26] did the ornate architectural carving that was beyond Church, whose ingenuity was sometimes a source of annoy-

In 1751 Paine supplied the richly carved doorcases for the Great Parlour (now Drawing Room), where William II hung his larger Grand Tour pictures

ance for Windham. 'I am very glad,' he wrote in April 1753, 'that Church makes so many pockets in my dressing room for I think there cannot be too many but I desire no fine conundrums of killing the devil and making places that in hard using will neither open nor shut.'[27]

In spite of their disagreements, Paine and Windham created a marvellous synthesis of architecture, decoration and furnishing cleverly attuned to the historic character of the house. Some owners would have wanted to modernise the south front and in so doing reduce the discord between it and the west wing. But not Windham, who responded warmly to its ancient charm in his treatment of its rooms. The Great Hall became sober, simplified neo-Tudor with plaster busts on brackets, and the Gothick bookcases of the new Library above it conveyed the same message of continuity with the ancient work. They housed a collection swelled by Windham's purchases in Italy, Geneva and the Low Countries, some of them bound by their owner (see p.68). The Stair Hall was also decorated with busts, as was the new Eating Room, which was hung with portraits of the previous two generations who had first built and furnished the west wing.

The delicately tinted plaster walls of the Great Hall, Stair Hall and Eating Room were a deliberate contrast with the sumptuous colour and gilding in the Great Parlour (now Drawing Room) and Cabinet beyond. Here, although the Caroline plasterwork was retained and embellished, Knowles's old panelling was removed to provide clear fields which could be hung with the trophies of Windham's Grand Tour. The newly papered walls of the Great Parlour were given over to Old Masters and in particular splendid marine pictures by the Van de Veldes and Samuel Scott. Those of the Cabinet, hung with damask, were dominated by the landscapes of Giovanni Battista Busiri: large oils of Tivoli, Frascati and Città Castellana, and little gouaches of monuments in the Roman countryside from which the sunshine still glows warmly after more than two centuries. Windham's intention of hanging the pictures in late 1751 was thwarted by the delayed arrival of the damask, and in January Mr Hall was asked to provide elevation drawings of the Cabinet and the Great Parlour for Windham in London so

that he could arrange the picture hang with paper cut-outs. The drawings survive for what is the earliest known hang to be documented in this way.

The work went on until January 1755, when Church fitted out the Library. A letter records the visit of one of Windham's friends from Common Room days, Thomas Dampier, at Christmas 1756:

If I owed you a Grudge, I could be well revenged upon you in my first Letter after the first visit to Felbrigg: I could cram you with compliments upon your House, Park &c, the Elegance and convenience, the *Utile Dulci*; the freedom and Ease; just enough Civility without Ceremony; the various Amusements for the Belly and Head from the Library to the Turning Wheel; above all, the Cheerfulness of mine Host and Hostess . . .[28]

Windham seems to have had no ambition other than to lead a full and active life and to make enjoyable use of his many gifts. He was never called upon to do otherwise, except when war came in 1756 and he became involved in the local militia at the instigation of his Norfolk friend and distant relative, the Hon. George Townshend. There were no readily available instructions for the training of the new militias so Windham gave much time to the production of *A Plan of Discipline, composed for the use of the Militia of the County of Norfolk* before its publication in 1759.[29]

Stillingfleet had written in the 1740s:

O born for active life! When shall I see
Thee, Windham, governing the grave debate,
'Midst the few pillars of the falling State
With sense acute and elocution free?[30]

But it has to be acknowledged that Felbrigg would be a less interesting house had Windham's energies been concentrated on a career rather than the creation of an ideal domestic environment. He died of consumption in October 1761 and it was soon to become evident that the ambitions which others had nursed for him were to be more than fulfilled by a brilliant son who had inherited many of his gifts.

The young William Windham was in his fourth year at Eton when his father died. 'Fighting Windham', as he was known to his fellows, could look

*A Bridge near Tivoli called Ponte del'Aqua Auria; by
G. B. Busiri. One of 32 views of Rome and its
surroundings acquired by William II while in Rome in
1739 or shortly afterwards. Most still hang in their original
positions in the Cabinet*

after himself. He had been placed under the care of
the Lower Master, his father's old friend Thomas
Dampier, who in 1766 was forced to send him
home for his prominent part in the school rebellion
against the unpopular new headmaster, Dr Foster.
At Oxford his self-discipline and capacity for work
were legendary; he enjoyed and retained throughout his life a remarkable facility in mathematics as
well as a wide and profound knowledge of classics.
But his emotional life was curiously unsatisfactory.

Having made the acquaintance of the attractive
Juliana Forrest and her equally alluring daughters,
on coming down from Oxford in 1770, he fell for
the eldest, Bridget, who was already married to
John Byng, the solitary traveller of the Torrington
Diaries, and for the next few years settled into a
debilitating regime of frustrated devotion. It was

not until 1775 that he began to develop an interest
in her sister Cecilia, whose unrequited feelings for
Windham's closest friend, George James Cholmondeley, were well known. Diaries record his
uneasy visits to Felbrigg in these years, when he
would stalk the empty rooms vainly trying to focus
on some worthwhile activity. The academic projects which he set himself were never sufficient to
retain his interest and it was only the cut and thrust
of national politics that were to inspire his great
powers of concentration and the eloquence for
which he was to have few rivals.

His political début was a memorable speech
against the continuation of the American War,
delivered at a public meeting in Norwich in 1778.
His neighbour Humphry Repton, the future landscape gardener, made a drawing of the youthful
Windham delivering the 'Norfolk Petition' which
he and his supporters drew up after the meeting had
gone against them. His first public post, in 1783 as
Chief Secretary to the Lord Lieutenant of Ireland
and Leader of the Irish House of Commons, was
cut short in a matter of months by illness. In 1784

he gained a seat in Parliament as the member for Norwich, with Repton, who had been his secretary in Ireland, as his election manager. Windham did not distinguish himself until 1788, when he helped mastermind the impeachment of Warren Hastings.

As a disciple of Edmund Burke, he had a particular horror of the French Revolution and when, in 1793, France declared war, Windham was a powerful advocate of a sustained and effective response. His group formed a coalition with Pitt's government in 1794 and Windham began a seven-year appointment as Secretary at War. When Pitt resigned because of the King's obstruction of Catholic Emancipation in the negotiations for the Act of Union in 1801, Windham followed him into opposition and attacked the new Addington administration over the flimsy peace which it made with Bonaparte at Amiens the same year. Britain was provoked into a fresh declaration of war in 1803 and Addington was soon swept from office. Pitt was back, but because he acceded to the King's exclusion of Fox from the government, Windham and his group declared their opposition to Pitt. Somewhat unfairly, this behaviour earned him the nickname 'Weathercock Windham', but his dissatisfaction with Pitt was given unfortunate expression when, after the Prime Minister's premature death in 1806, Windham argued doggedly in Parliament against a public funeral and a monument in Westminster Abbey. He gained responsibility for the army again in the short-lived 'Ministry of all the Talents', headed by Grenville, and as Secretary for War and the Colonies he made enduring and valuable reforms in army pay and conditions, but did little of value in the field of strategy.

In 1775 Windham had put Felbrigg under the care of Nathaniel Kent, who already had a reputation as an agent and agricultural improver, and during Kent's period much planting as well as the enclosure of common land took place (see p.88). That the great politician made only a slight impression on the house is explained partly by his father's extensive remodelling and partly by his own inscrutable personal life. He married Cecilia Forrest as late as 1798 when they were both in their late forties and there was no prospect of a young family demanding changes or successors to enjoy them.

William Windham III (1750–1810) delivering his first important political speech, in Norwich in 1778. This drawing is by his aide, the future landscape gardener Humphry Repton

The inventories which he conscientiously drew up on his coming of age in 1771 are an invaluable record of his father's eighteenth-century interiors.[31] Between 1773 and 1777 he made a few small changes of his own[32] and in 1788–9 the architect Robert Furze Brettingham was commissioned to make alterations. The closing-up of the west window of the Great Hall, the replacement of the Cabinet fireplace, the creation of a new butler's pantry and the addition of waterclosets are all documented, as is the fact that Windham's passion for learning required that the west window of the Library be sacrificed to new bookpresses.[33] Light levels in the Library were further reduced by Brettingham's coloured glass in Gothic framing. 'The gloom thrown into the apartment by the deep projecting munnions, the painted windows, and the sombre hue of the wainscot, renders it a retirement truly adapted to study', as an early nineteenth-century guidebook writer was to observe.[34] His old friend Repton returned in 1806 to replace Paine's staircase lantern, and Brettingham's scheme for the new Morning Room, which finally replaced the old kitchen at the east end of the south front, was carried out in 1809.

None of this work could be described as an urgent necessity, which may explain why, in November 1793, Windham should have written to the dilatory James Wyatt in the following terms over an unspecified project at Felbrigg rather than simply hire another architect:

I have written to you no less than five letters desiring to know, whether you meant to do this or not; and you have returned no answer,

. . . Pray, Sir, who are you, upon whom engagements are to be of no force; and who are to set aside all forms of civility, established between man and man? Had the most private gentleman of the country written to the first minister of the country, he would have received an answer in a quarter of the time. And what is this privilege denied to persons in that station, which you suppose to be possessed by you? A privilege not allowed to a man's betters, may be suspected to be one, of which he has no great reason to boast. But of this I leave you to judge.[35]

This drubbing had no effect on Wyatt but it gives an idea of Windham's powers as an orator and of the intellectual obstinacy which could enslave him to a lost cause. Its stylish invective is almost worthy of his friend Samuel Johnson, whose bedside he attended during the sage's final illness in 1784. The kindness and consideration Windham showed to Johnson then were examples of the unswerving loyalty which he could give to his true friends. The Library still contains some of Johnson's books, which were given during the old man's last days as keepsakes in recognition of Windham's devotion to learning. These two facets of Windham's character, and the physical courage learnt in his youth, were also displayed in the incident which led to his death on 4 June 1810. A painful malignancy on his hip, which required an agonising and fatal operation, was the result of an injury which he sustained while courageously saving the library of his friend Frederick North from a blazing house.

NOTES

1 NNRO, WKC 6/14.

2 Ibid.

3 NNRO, WKC 7/21.

4 NNRO, WKC 5/192.

5 NNRO, WKC 5/163. January 1691: 'pd the Smith for Window barrs for the parlor pt 1.0.0.'

6 NNRO, WKC 6/16.

7 NNRO, WKC 6/14 f.88v.

8 See J. Maddison, 'Architectural Drawings at Blickling Hall', *Architectural History*, xxxiv, 1991, p.75.

9 NNRO, WKC 7/21.

10 NNRO, WKC 5/197.

11 NNRO, WKC 5/189, 191 and 192.

12 NNRO, WKC 6/29.

13 NNRO, WKC 7/155.

14 NNRO, WKC 6/23.

15 Ibid.

16 *Felbrigg*, pp.110–11.

17 Ibid., p.116–17 for a fuller quotation.

18 NNRO, WKC 7/178/4.

19 NNRO, WKC 7/52.

20 NNRO, WKC 5/217, 219.

21 NNRO, WKC 7/178/6.

22 See *Felbrigg*, pp.126–7, 131–2.

23 NNRO, WKC 7/179/I.

24 NNRO, WKC 7/179/11.

25 These drawings are NNRO, WKC 6/460. Bladwell received £448 in July 1756 (NNRO, WKC 6/453).

26 Quintin was being paid for carving and gilding at Felbrigg between March 1751 and May 1753 (NNRO, WKC 5/219).

27 NNRO, WKC 7/179/19. For a summary of Church's work, see NNRO, WKC 5/217.

28 *Felbrigg*, p.145.

29 See J. A. Houlding, *Fit for Service: The Training of the British Army 1715–1795*, p.207.

30 *Felbrigg*, p.125, where the full sonnet is given.

31 NNRO, WKC 6/455. The inventory of the rooms is undated but is clearly contemporary with the linen inventory (NNRO, WKC 6/463), which is dated June 1771.

32 See bill of Charles Rice of North Walsham for beds, festoon window curtains, repair of Chinese wallpaper, etc. (NNRO, WKC 6/96).

33 NNRO, WKC 7/98/1–21 and WKC 6/150/61.

34 E. Bartell Jr, *Cromer Considered as a Watering Place*, 1806, p.63.

35 BM, Add. MS 37914 f.67.

CHAPTER FIVE
THE LAST TWO CENTURIES

Windham had first thought of leaving Felbrigg to one of his close circle of friends but in the end settled it upon William, the eldest son of his half-brother George Lukin, who had been rector of Felbrigg and was now Dean of Wells. William and his brothers are shown in a marvellous group portrait by William Bigg, setting off from Felbrigg Parsonage for a day's shooting, surrounded by their servants and dogs. A distinguished sailor, whose life before the mast began in 1781 at the age of thirteen, William Lukin was to make his reputation in 1806 as the captain of the *Mars*, which, in an action off Rochefort, helped to capture four French troop ships. In the following year the *Mars* took part in the bombardment of Copenhagen and it was around this time that Cotman made his famous watercolour of Lukin's ship at anchor off Cromer. Lukin became a Vice-Admiral before he left the navy in 1814. The widowed Cecilia Windham, who now spent much of her time away from Norfolk, had a life interest in Felbrigg, which meant that he could not enter into his inheritance until her death. So the Admiral bided his time with visibly increasing impatience in Felbrigg Parsonage, the boyhood home where he had been able to live since the removal of the rector to Metton.

With Cecilia Windham's passing in 1824, Lukin was now required to assume the name and arms of Windham as a surrogate heir. The house was woken from its fourteen years of slumber by a swift and sudden campaign of alterations by W.J. Donthorn, a local architect who at his best could produce work of great originality and power.[1] At this period Felbrigg's informality, its charming accretion of different periods and styles and the mixture of materials which today we find so endearing, would not have been admired. Donthorn's first plan, which involved a grand north dining-room, the remodelling of the service wing

and the building of stables in Tuscan Doric, was, like Samwell's first effort, turned down. The dining-room was not wanted and the style of the stables better suited to Nash's London, was evidently considered inappropriate. In the event Donthorn was allowed to remodel Paine's service arcade as a passage with Gothick windows and pavilions at either end. The stable block rose to the east in castellated neo-Tudor and the whole of this significantly extended south front was given a coat of lime render, lined out to look like masonry.[2] This work was completed with great expedition and perhaps too much economy in 1825, and some years later in 1831 the Admiral remedied the main deficiency of the Dining Room by building what is now known as the Bird Corridor along the back of the south block to improve communication with the Kitchen.

The interior of the house was much enriched during these years. The family brought back sea pictures by Abraham Storck and Bakhuysen from their prolonged visit to Belgium in 1820–1. The elegant eighteenth-century rooms with their mahogany and walnut furniture were now augmented with new pieces: a billiard-table for the Great Hall, a new gilt and damask suite for the Great Parlour (which now became the Drawing Room) and some handsome four-posters for the bedrooms. The Regency taste for inlaid furniture expressed itself in some ingenious tables of rosewood and mahogany decorated with brass, and in the acquisition of French Boulle writing-tables and pedestals, the best of which is the splendid late seventeenth-century *bureau Mazarin* now in the Cabinet. All these pieces are recorded in the inventory taken at the Admiral's death in 1833.[3]

His eldest son, William Howe Windham, had been born in 1802. He was away on the Grand Tour in 1824–5 and returned to a house strikingly

*Captain William Lukin (1768–1833) and his brothers
setting off from Felbrigg Parsonage for a day's shooting; by
William Redmore Bigg, 1803 (Morning Room). Lukin
inherited Felbrigg from his uncle, William Windham III,
whose surname he adopted when he moved into the house
in 1824*

transformed. He was to become a model improving landlord who, under the inspiration of Coke of
Holkham, invested heavily in the farms, renewing
their buildings, and punctiliously recording their
construction with date stones in the gables (his
alterations to the hall were recorded in the same
way). He rose to county prominence as a Whig
member for Norfolk in 1832, but lost his seat in
1837. It was perhaps with a politician's eye to self-
advertisement that he put up two new pairs of

lodges in the early 1840s, the grandest of which
were built facing Cromer, by then a very fashionable resort, from which genteel tourists would
make a bee-line for the hall. Although the mortgages taken out to finance the purchase of the
nearby Hanworth estate prevented him from
making extensive renovations to the house, he did
spend considerable sums on its most public room,
the Great Hall. William Windham II's stripped
Gothic interior with its little plaster busts, already
substantially remodelled by William Windham III,
gave place to an early Victorian scheme with
gargantuan neo-Jacobean details in which marble
busts of past and present Whig heroes stood on
plinths.

The windows were filled with stained glass both
new and ancient, and in the new heraldic panels

The Great Hall, which was remodelled in the 1840s by William Howe Windham, who added the neo-Jacobean doorcases and ceiling

which decorated the reopened west window the squire celebrated his marriage, in 1835, to the daughter of the 1st Marquess of Bristol, Lady Sophia Hervey, whose family home, Ickworth in Suffolk, is now also in the care of the National Trust.[4] The male members of Lady Sophia's family had a reputation for a certain eccentricity in looks and behaviour that stretched back to the early eighteenth century. She herself was highly strung and her new husband's habit of shouting, whistling and singing to himself while alone in the Drawing Room was later remarked upon by the servants. So it was not perhaps entirely surprising that their son, who was born in 1840, turned into something of an oddity.

William Frederick, who acquired the nickname 'Mad Windham' in the merciless climate of Victorian Eton, was certainly retarded, and was further handicapped by his upbringing. His passion for uniform was encouraged in early childhood when his parents gave him a little suit of the blue and red livery which the Felbrigg servants had worn since

Ashe Windham's day. He was allowed to wait at table and spent his time in the Servants' Hall. As he grew up he became interested in trains and, having acquired a guard's uniform, could be found on the platforms of local stations causing chaos with unauthorised whistle blasts. His father died in 1854 and in due course Lady Sophia found consolation in the arms of Signor Giubilei, an Italian opera singer whom she had met in Torquay on an extended tour of watering places. Her son's education was neglected and in the absence of parental affection his eccentricities became more pronounced.[5]

This innocent came of age in 1861 and made his way to London where he dressed up as a policeman and patrolled the Haymarket, rounding up the dubious women who poured out of the pubs at closing time and urging the regular force to accompany them to the station. In the same year, on a visit to Ascot, he fell into the clutches of Agnes Willoughby, a glamorous kept woman whose protector, the timber contractor and notorious pimp 'Mahogany' Roberts, was soon to take an unhealthy interest in the Felbrigg woods. Agnes was a striking figure who sported a scarlet riding mantle at meetings of the Royal Buckhounds and was perpetually surrounded by crowds of admiring officers. Her blond hair and china doll complexion captivated Windham, as did the epithet 'pretty horsebreaker' which she and her kind attracted.

It was a perilous moment for Felbrigg and desperate measures were required when Windham assented to a generous marriage settlement which guaranteed an income for Agnes. His uncle, General Charles Windham, the bearded Crimean War hero of the assault on the Redan in 1855, found himself in an extremely awkward position. He wanted to protect the estate and its family from impending ruin but was compromised by his sons' interest as heirs. His petition for *De Lunatico Inquirendo*, to establish that his nephew was barred from entering into any marriage settlement, led to a notorious inquiry which sat for 34 days, heard the evidence of 140 witnesses, provided employment for a string of prominent lawyers and made a marvellous spectacle for the press. The most convincing witnesses, including servants from Felbrigg and Eton tutors, were sympathetic to Windham. When their evidence and that of Windham himself, who gave a creditable performance, was set against the exaggerated claims of the General's all too fallible witnesses, the case collapsed and Windham was declared sane.

The marriage was predictably short-lived and Agnes soon fled from a husband she had always found distasteful to an old flame (coincidentally another Italian singer), returning only for two brief reconciliations, one of which she used to obtain the reversion of the Hanworth estate for the child with whom she was now pregnant. Windham's debts were completely out of control. The estate passed into the hands of his banker and was bought in 1863 by a Norwich merchant, John Ketton, who had made a fortune from oil-cake and cattle feed in the 1830s and '40s and altered his name from Kitton in 1853. 'Windham is gone to the dogs. Felbrigg has gone to the Kittens,' as the Rev. B. J. Armstrong recorded in his diary for January 1864.[6]

Before his death in 1866 Windham remained a conspicuous figure in north Norfolk. He bought a mail van, had it painted scarlet, with the Windham arms, and drove it daily into Norwich for his letters. Then he became the owner and driver of a coach which travelled established routes, pinching the customers of other companies and giving them free trips until, after he had lost everything, he concluded with a spell as an increasingly erratic and dangerous driver of the express coach between Cromer and Norwich.

The Kettons made surprisingly little impact on Felbrigg. They moved in during March 1863 and lived happily in the old house with all its contents and memories for many years, and today there is almost no sign of them. John Ketton, who became rather cantankerous in later years, disinherited his elder son and the estate passed to the younger brother Robert on his death in 1872. Robert Ketton's two youngest sisters, Marion and

William Frederick Windham (1840–66) – 'Mad Windham'; from a photograph c.1862

Gertrude, kept house for him. There are photographs of the Ketton girls sitting about in the rooms, playing billiards and enacting ghostly apparitions with clever double exposures. When first one sister and then the other died prematurely in the 1890s, Robert Ketton was devastated, and relapsed into a reclusive lifestyle in which the house and estate fell into decay. The few repairs that were done were met from the sale of assets and in 1918 and 1919 Ketton put some of the treasures of the house on the market, including Bladwell's splendid chairs and sofas from the Cabinet, some of the most important books from the Library and much of the porcelain.

Within five years he gave up and made over Felbrigg to his nephew, Wyndham Cremer, whose grandmother had been a Cromer Wyndham, descended from the younger brother of the builder of the house. Like Lukin, he was now required, as a condition of inheritance, to add another name to his own and so become Wyndham Ketton-Cremer. He had married Emily Bayly in 1905 and had only

recently moved, in 1920, to Beeston Hall, north-west of Felbrigg. The Cremers had two sons, of whom the elder, Robert Wyndham Ketton-Cremer, was destined to become the last and most learned squire of Felbrigg.

The Cremers gave up an altogether manageable and agreeable house at Beeston and it says much for their sense of duty that they were prepared to take on the challenge of Felbrigg. The sale of some farms and of a few further contents including furniture and an important picture by Van Goyen, enabled the most formidable repairs to be tackled at the house and at the church, which was now virtually a ruin with:

Holes in the roof, green slime dripping down the walls, windows broken, doors rotting, jackdaws and bats befouling everything. The great monument to Thomas Windham had grown so insecure that the rector would never venture near it, even at moments of the service when the rubric required him to do so.[7]

Shortly after his father inherited the estate in 1924, Robert Wyndham Ketton-Cremer went up

The Ketton family in the Drawing Room in the 1870s

to Balliol. Here he suffered an attack of the rheumatic fever which had already plagued him at Harrow. His mother had to leave the preoccupations of Felbrigg and nurse him back to health but he was left with a weak heart and with limited use of his right hand, and in later life he was rendered susceptible to a series of increasingly serious illnesses. These problems are made light of in Ketton-Cremer's account of the later history of Felbrigg in a characteristically stoical manner. He wrote little about himself in *Felbrigg: The Story of a House*, but a powerful sense of the man comes across in the writing. His real interest was in people and in what happened to them. He treated them with humanity and understanding in his daily dealings as in his fine books (see Bibliography). His biographies of *Horace Walpole* (1940) and *Thomas Gray* (1955) are highly regarded and he gave up a project to write the life of Matthew Prior in order to tackle *Felbrigg*. He soaked himself in the culture and particularly the literature of the eighteenth century. His brilliant use of the essay and his economical but lyrical descriptive prose with its penetrating understatements and beautifully balanced sentences display his sensitivity to those early writers.

Respect for established institutions was reflected in old-fashioned Conservative politics, and a wariness of radicalism is plainly evident in his writing. He played, as his predecessors had done, a full part in the life of his county. As High Sheriff of Norfolk in 1951–2 he was required to witness two hangings and as a JP he administered justice. His thorough knowledge of Norfolk churches made him an ideal chairman of the Norwich Diocesan Advisory Committee, and he was actively involved in the founding of the University of East Anglia, which conferred an honorary D. Litt on him in 1969, and to which he bequeathed his working library of books on Norfolk history. But he did not relish public prominence:

Wyndham, as he was only too ready to admit, was a shy man, and this was reflected in his conversation by the fact that he seldom ever looked anyone straight in the face; the glance from his large brown eyes always seemed to be sliding away from one. But there was nothing shy about his delivery, which flowed as smoothly as the Danube. . . . It was certainly a voice

Robert Wyndham Ketton-Cremer (1906–69), the last squire of Felbrigg, which he bequeathed to the National Trust; by Allan Gwynne-Jones, 1969–70 (Great Hall)

that gave one the impression of having been nurtured on vintage port rather then on dry martinis.[8]

His quiet demeanour could sometimes give way to anger. The explosion when a guest inconvenienced his staff by coming down late for dinner is recounted by Sir Brinsley Ford, and others wince at the memory of his wrath when he discovered someone smoking a cigarette in Felbrigg church. Devout Christianity was central to him and this, combined with a sense of duty inculcated by his parents, gave him a formidable strength of character. As Mary Lascelles remarked, 'He was not merely consistent, he was all of a piece throughout.'[9]

After his father's death in 1933, he became his own land agent and for many years ran the estate single-handed, carefully balancing the needs of the house against those of his tenants. He restrained the urge to clean important pictures when he knew that the money was more urgently needed for the improvement of cottages, and found it necessary in 1934 to sell the best of William Windham II's splendid Van de Veldes to the National Maritime Museum. In the hall and its gardens architectural

35

repairs were the most pressing priority. In 1937 he restored the Dove-house and in 1958 he tackled the Orangery, which had been derelict since 1900. His architect was Donovan Purcell and it was he who designed the simple mahogany lamp standards which were introduced into most of the rooms when electricity reached the hall in 1954. This was long after the estate workers' cottages had been supplied, and Sir Brinsley Ford recalled his early visits to Felbrigg in the 1950s, when one read by oil lamps and went to bed by candlelight.

The Felbrigg landscape meant as much to him as the house, and he loved trees. This is as evident from the extent and variety of his plantations as it is in the way that he writes about the estate management of the early Windhams. It was in the setting of his woods that Sir Brinsley Ford gives us a picture of 'the Squire', as he was locally known, in 1963:

I have written in my Journal that as I walked behind Wyndham on that September afternoon '. . . his portly figure made even more shapeless by an old mackintosh, his grey hair straggling onto his collar beneath a green pork-pie hat, his slightly gouty step supported by a walking stick, I was not unaware that I was treading in the wake of one who already ranks as one of Norfolk's worthies, and whose memory will be treasured for years to come.'[10]

Wyndham Ketton-Cremer did not marry and the central tragedy of his life was the loss of his younger brother Dick in the German invasion of Crete in May 1941. He writes about it most movingly at the end of The Story of a House and the last two chapters are characterised by sadness and a wistful uncertainty about the future. Others felt it too and the less sensitive would sometimes ask him what he was going to do with Felbrigg. Beeston, which had been settled on his brother, had become a preparatory school, but to any inquiries about Felbrigg, the Squire would respond gravely that it was to be left to a cats' home. In fact he had already made an approach to the National Trust in 1941 and its Executive Committee had accepted the property on merit, subject to satisfactory financial arrangements. He had been involved in the work of the National Trust since the late 1940s, when he had helped Alec Penrose, the Honorary Regional Representative, with decisions about the decoration of the Orangery at Blickling, and he became a most conscientious and valued member of its Regional Committee. On his death in December 1969 Felbrigg and all its wonderful contents, its woods, its parkland and its farms were formally offered to the Trust.

His will had required that the Trust accept or refuse the property within six months of his death and, as soon as it had been agreed with the executors that a number of outlying properties could be sold to fund its future care, the core of the Felbrigg estate passed into the Trust's hands for permanent preservation. The house was opened to the public almost immediately. At this stage they were allowed to see only the ground-floor rooms. Then after careful cleaning and cataloguing it was possible to open the Library and eventually the bedrooms of the west front, which had been closed up because of their unsafe floors and the danger which they posed to the remarkable ceilings beneath. The repair of these rooms and of the stable block were the only large-scale works undertaken by the Trust in the 1970s. The Squire's prudent estate management and his conscientious care of the building had left no heavy burdens for its new owners, other than the obligation to follow his example.

NOTES

1 R. O'Donnel, 'W. J. Donthorn (1799–1859)', Architectural History, xxi, 1978, pp.83–92.

2 Donthorn's letters are NNRO, WKC 7/97.

3 NNRO, WKC 6/471.

4 William White, Directory of Norfolk, 1845, recorded 'Mr W. has recently . . . filled the great hall windows with stained glass brought from Belgium'.

5 The story is recounted in D. MacAndrew, 'Mr and Mrs Windham', The Saturday Book, 1951.

6 B. J. Armstrong, A Norfolk Diary, ed. H. B. J. Armstrong, 1949, p.109.

7 Felbrigg, p.284.

8 Sir Brinsley Ford, 'Staying at Felbrigg as a Guest of Wyndham Ketton-Cremer', National Trust Year Book, 1977–8, p.60.

9 M. Lascelles, 'Robert Wyndham Ketton-Cremer, 1906–1969', Proceedings of the British Academy, lvi, 1970, p.403ff.

10 Sir Brinsley Ford, op. cit., p.58.

CHAPTER SIX

TOUR OF THE HOUSE

The Exterior

THE SOUTH FRONT

This, the earliest part of the house, was begun in about 1620 and incorporates remains of the previous Tudor house. The four-centred heads of old cellar windows were found in the plinth to the right of the front door during recent repairs. It is built of a mixture of brick, flint and pebble with dressings in a fine oolitic Ketton limestone from Northamptonshire. The arms above the entrance are those of Sir John Wyndham (1558–1645), of Orchard Wyndham in Somerset, impaling those of Joan Portman, his wife, and of their son Thomas Windham (1585–1654) and his first wife Elizabeth Lytton, whom he married in 1620.

The design has much in common with the architecture of Blickling Hall, which was being built simultaneously, and many of the details are identical, as were some of the craftsmen (see p.9). The strongly projecting bay windows are the same as those of Blickling's east front and the mouldings of their mullions could have been cut from the same template. The Great Hall lies to the left of the porch, and behind the bay window to the right originally lay the kitchen and pantry. Renaissance symmetry demanded that state rooms and domestic offices received identical expression. Above the Great Hall on the first floor was probably the Great Chamber (replaced in the 1750s by the Library). The location of the other Jacobean rooms is uncertain, but if there was a Long Gallery at Felbrigg, it was probably in the attic, which had, until earlier in the present century, three dormer windows which are recorded in early photographs and which are shown with Dutch gables in eighteenth-century prints. The fact that a handsome late seventeenth-century family staircase at the rear of this front rises to the attic would also argue for an important room on the top floor. The upper part of the front was

being completed in 1624, when the stone lions on the gables were provided. The inscription 'Gloria Deo in Excelsis' may relate to the satisfactory re-establishment of the Windhams at Felbrigg by Sir John Wyndham of Orchard after a period of decline and misfortune in which the Norfolk branch died out (see p.10). The sundial may have been an addition of the 1750s. Its decorative iron gnomon is similar to the ironwork of James Paine's staircase.

The front was rendered by W.J.Donthorn for Admiral Windham in about 1825 and beneath this protective coating, which is gradually deteriorating, are substantial traces of earlier treatments. The earliest layer is red wash with white mortar lining out, a fictive brickwork effect which is typical of much sixteenth- and early seventeenth-century architecture. Above this is a layer of ochre wash, which may be early eighteenth-century, and then white, which appears to be referred to in the correspondence of the 1750s.

THE EAST FRONT

This reveals the substantial extension to the rear of the Jacobean house built by William Windham I in 1675 (see p.12). It copied the side gables of the Jacobean front but was entirely of brick. The east bay was altered by William Windham III in 1809 (see p.29), when William Collins made alterations to the rooms on this side.

THE EAST WING

This service wing was built by James Paine for William Windham II in 1749 and replaced a narrower range which his father Ashe had built by about 1710 (see p.23). Paine's design was Palladian in character: a pedimented centre and semicircular 'therm' windows, with an open arcade in front described in letters as a 'piazza'. In 1825 Donthorn remodelled the arcade, built the pavilions and remodelled the open walk with Gothick windows to make a corridor.

THE STABLE BLOCK

Built in 1824–5 for Admiral Windham by Donthorn, whose first idea had been a classical design with a screen of Tuscan columns along the front. The neo-Tudor scheme was, like much architecture of this period, more monumental in conception than in execution and in its original state the brick structure relied on a render coating in which string courses, window hoods and other details were modelled over brick and tile armatures. Nearly all of this render has fallen off since about 1900. The screen, a similar notion to the much finer one which Wilkins put up at King's College, Cambridge in 1824–8, closes a courtyard which had carriage houses in the centre flanked by wings containing stalls and loose boxes. The right-hand wing was converted many years ago into a house and the left-hand one, deprived long-since of its stable fittings, was used by the gardeners. In 1989 the carriage houses were converted into a restaurant by the National Trust and in 1993 the two

wings became an additional cafeteria and the shop. The removal of the latter to this position enabled the east wing and its important servants' rooms and workshops to be shown to the public in a suitable manner. The stalls in the north-west corner have been restored and the loose box in which Dick Ketton-Cremer (see p.36) kept his horse, Jester, has been preserved.

THE WEST FRONT

Designs for the extension of the Jacobean house were presented to William Windham I in 1674 by the gentleman architect William Samwell (see p.15). Samwell died in 1675 and it appears that the building of this new front was not tackled until the mid-1680s. The right-hand lead rainwater head is dated 1686. The extension absorbed the rear portion of the Jacobean house. Its beautifully proportioned classicism and superb brickwork make an arresting contrast with the old front, but the difference may have been less at first if the earlier work retained its red colourwash. Samwell's elevation drawing shows a figure of Hercules standing in a niche between the two central first-floor windows and the texture of the brickwork here suggests that such a feature may once have existed. On the ground floor, the new

Felbrigg from the south-west

building contained a stair hall (with an external door), the Great Parlour and at the north (left-hand) end a smaller Drawing Room. The first floor contained a large ante-room linked to a bed-chamber and a couple of closets.

The front has undergone a number of changes. The slate roof replaced the original covering in August 1751, when William Kilner was paid for the freight of 40 tons of Westmorland slate from Hawkshead to Cromer. The pedimented dormers are also of this date, replacing similar features whose pediments were alternately curved and triangular. At the same time the polygonal bay was put up at the north end and a two-storey addition for corridors added at the rear (see p.24). Partly because William Samwell is known to have pioneered the use of sash windows in his 1675 front at Ham House in Surrey, it is tempting to see the thickly barred sashes as early features, but they are more likely to be early eighteenth-century. Samwell's drawing showed mullion-and-transom windows and there is evidence that the Great Parlour had them (see p.18). The sashes of the four northern windows of the first floor could be as early as 1704 (see p.18). Others may have been introduced in 1728 when Katherine Windham wrote to her son Ashe, 'The Coll [Ashe's brother Colonel William Windham] has seen the Sashes and says they are very nicely done.' The thick glazing bars of these windows were copied in William Windham II's additions of the 1750s, notably in the first-floor windows of the north bay. The thinner and more elegant sash bars of some of the other windows can probably be connected with the purchase of new sash weights by William Windham III in 1789, which would have been especially necessary in the Great Parlour where the openings were now filled by single frames which slid upwards into a wall cavity.

THE ORANGERY

This building was contemplated as early as 1694 (see p.18) and it was more or less complete by 1707 (see p.20). Ashe Windham was probably the designer of this austere paraphrase of the architecture of the west wing and the drawings show that it had tall sash windows originally. The lawn in front of it was known as the Greenhouse garden in the mid-eighteenth century and it is here that the orange trees would have stood in formal patterns during

the warm weather. In the nineteenth century the building was given a glass roof, which by 1958 had completely rotted away and in this year both roof and cornice were completely reconstructed from the old drawings by R. W. Ketton-Cremer. It now contains some splendid camellias, which were planted in the nineteenth century.

THE NORTH FRONT

This view of the house was opened up by Ashe Windham in the early eighteenth century when he demolished two service ranges which ran across it (see p.20). They were replaced by the service courtyard to the east whose plain back wall, relieved by recessed brick panels similar to those on the back of the Orangery, formed one side of a new 'Parlour Garden'. The rear wall of the 1675 extension of the south front is plainly visible from here, as is the back of the 1680s west wing with its substantial extensions of 1751. The latter very much impinged on Ashe's Parlour Garden, which was further reduced in 1831, when Admiral Windham built what is now known as the Bird Corridor, to improve communication between the Kitchen and the Dining Room.

THE GRASS COURTYARD

The courtyard and its buildings are visible from the Kitchen, from the windows of the east wing and from the path next to the west side of the stable block. A number of dwellings were formed in its north range by Ketton-Cremer, and the courtyard is now used by the residents. The earliest portion of Ashe Windham's service yard (see p.20) is the west range, where the rubbed brick arches of some of the small ground-floor windows are clearly early eighteenth-century. This range was first built to accommodate a servants' hall, kitchen, bakehouse and meat room. The tall round-headed windows of the present Kitchen are probably William Windham III's modifications, as are those of the first floor. A common plinth runs along the north range, which in Ashe's time contained the dairy, wash-house, malt-house and brew-house, but much of this was rebuilt in the later eighteenth century. The dairy and wash-house end was altered by the last squire towards the end of his life and became his winter quarters, known as 'The Retreat'. The east side has the granary, a miraculously unaltered building of about 1710, with leaded windows, louvred ventilators and stout doors. The north wall of the east wing of 1749–50 (see p.24) closes the south side of the courtyard and here one can see unaltered some of the typically Palladian details of Paine's original design, as well as an addition at the west end of 1851.

The Interior

THE PORCH AND SCREENS PASSAGE

The Porch is spanned by a Jacobean Gothic rib vault whose boss displays the Windham arms surrounded by the fetterlock badge they took over from the Felbriggs. The inner archway is mid-nineteenth-century and its mutilated predecessor is to be seen in the Walled Garden. Beyond lies the passage formed originally by the screen of the Jacobean Great Hall. In those days there would have been at least two doors on the right to the pantry, butteries and servery. The blank arch at the end is Jacobean.

FURNITURE

Two oval, gilt-framed mirrors, early nineteenth-century.

Six oak hall chairs and four walnut armchairs, all decorated with the Windham crest, from the 1750s furnishing of the Great Hall.

SCULPTURE

? ITALIAN, early nineteenth-century
Reduction of the Farnese Hercules
White marble, on a columnar plinth of grey and white marble, incorporating the foreparts of Egyptian lions. It was probably installed here by William Howe Windham around 1840.

THE LOBBY

This area, a pantry until the early nineteenth century, has a low ceiling like the Screens Passage, preserving an ancient mezzanine level which

Thomas Wyndham of Cromer, writing in 1745, described as 'the Master's Room wch command'd the Kitchen and Hall and had for its base the Butterys.... No Commandant was ever better lodged in any citadel, to defend his Outworks than your Predecessors in their Metzinino between the two Halls, where meat was both dress'd and devour'd.' This was perhaps the 'eying chamber' mentioned in the Jacobean building accounts.

PICTURES

Bad pastiches of Canaletto (the four *Views of the Grand Canal in Venice*) and Van der Heyden (the *View of the Gate to a Dutch Town*), and naïve *Views of Cromer* (an early eighteenth-century oil, and an ink-and-watercolour sketch of c.1800–10, optimistically attributed by Ketton-Cremer to John Thirtle).

BRONZE SCULPTURE

? GERMAN, ? seventeenth-century
Hercules with his club and an apple of the Hesperides

R. & S. GARRARD, after EDMUND COTTERELL (b.1795, exh. 1822–58)
Equestrian statuette of the Duke of Wellington (1769–1852)
Published 18 June 1851, apparently to meet the demand arising from the recrudescence in the 'Iron Duke's' popularity around the time of the Great Exhibition.

FURNITURE

Late seventeenth-century oyster veneer glove box, sitting on a small table of c.1715.

Octagonal Neo-classical iron strong box, c.1780.

Drop-leaf gaming table, c.1730.

A handsome side-table of c.1730, grained to resemble mahogany, with a marble slab.

Drop-leaf oval mahogany gaming table with spade feet, c.1780.

CERAMICS

Four blue-and-white vases. One pair has the Kangxi mark (1662–1722) and is of the period, the others are late Ming (c.1640, known as Transitional) *rolwagens* (tall cylindrical vases), similar to those Queen Mary used to decorate the Water Gallery, Hampton Court, c.1690.

THE MORNING ROOM

This was the kitchen of the Jacobean house and in the mid-eighteenth century was considered as a possible dining-room. It remained in service use until 1809, when William Collins is known to have provided designs for the 'East Parlour windows'. It was panelled out at this time and painted in tones of off-white. The present scheme may date from the mid-nineteenth century.

FIREPLACE

White marble, c.1850. Steel and brass fender of c.1820 with contemporary irons.

PICTURES

LEFT OF DOOR:

GEORGE CLINT, ARA (1770–1854)
Maria Augusta (Lukin) Windham, Mrs George Wyndham (1805–71)
Oval
Painted in 1824, the year that her father, the Admiral, changed his name from Lukin to Windham, and two years before she married George Wyndham of Cromer Hall (descendant of a younger son of Sir John Wyndham of Orchard Wyndham).

WILLIAM EDWARD WEST (1788–1857)
Anne Thellusson, Mrs William (Lukin) Windham (1775–1849)
Daughter of Peter Thellusson of Brodsworth, and wife of Vice-Admiral (Lukin) Windham. Painted in 1833, the last year of this American artist's sojourn in England.

LEFT OF CHIMNEY-PIECE:

ENGLISH, nineteenth-century
Two portraits of William Howe Windham (1802–54)
The eldest son and heir of Admiral (Lukin) Windham, in black and white chalks and in oils, at about the ages of 40 and 50 respectively. The portrait in oils may be posthumous. The sitter is best known for his enlargement and improvement of the Felbrigg estate.

NEAR LEFT AND RIGHT OF CHIMNEY-PIECE:

ENGLISH, c.1700
Cobbler and client and *Friar and fair penitent*
Panel
Typical English imitations of Dutch seventeenth-century paintings – more particularly, of those painted by the Dutch immigrant Egbert van Heemskerk (c.1635–1704), especially in the anti-clerical slant given to one of them.

THOMAS WORLIDGE (1700–66)
Abraham and Isaac and ? *Polish nobleman*
Etchings. Dated 1752 and ? 1752
Characteristic examples of Rembrandt imitations by this interesting amateur painter and etcher.

OVER CHIMNEY-PIECE:

WILLIAM REDMORE BIGG, RA (1755–1828)
Captain Lukin and his brothers setting off shooting, with Cawston the gamekeeper
Inscribed on the back as painted by Bigg in 1803
The shooting party is setting off from Felbrigg Parsonage (now demolished), where the Lukins' father lived until his death in 1812, and where Admiral Lukin lived until he moved into the Hall in 1824. Bigg is better known as a genre painter than as an artist of sporting pictures and conversation pieces, so the gamekeeper comes off best. Captain (later Vice-Admiral) Lukin stands in the centre, flanked by his brothers Robert and George. John, astride a horse, was later to marry John Sell Cotman and Ann Miles in Felbrigg church, seen in the distance.

ENGLISH, c.1800
Captain William Lukin (later Vice-Admiral Windham) (1768–1833)
Painted before he succeeded to Felbrigg and took the name of Windham, this has been attributed to Sir William Beechey (1753–1839).

MID-RIGHT OF CHIMNEY-PIECE:

ENGLISH, c.1855
Lady Sophia (Hervey) Windham (1811–63)
Daughter of the 1st Marquess of Bristol, married in 1835 to William Howe Windham (on the other side of the chimney-piece). Apparently painted as his widow, before her second marriage, in 1858, to Signor Giubilei (see p.32).

FAR RIGHT OF CHIMNEY-PIECE:

After CHARLES CATTON, RA (1728–98)
Self-portrait of the Artist
Watercolour
A copy of the *Self-portrait* in oils now in the Yale Center for British Art. Though better known as a landscape painter (eg of *Happisburgh Beach* here), Catton also painted animals and portraits, and is shown with a painting of a lion.

LEFT OF WINDOW BAY:

ENGLISH, mid-nineteenth-century
Frederick William Hervey, 1st Marquess of Bristol
(1769–1859)
Son of the Earl-Bishop of Bristol and Derry, whom
he succeeded in 1803, when he was Under-Sec-
retary of State for Foreign Affairs, following the
resignation of Pitt and William Windham III in
1801. Father of Lady Sophia (Hervey) Windham
(see p.41). This may be a posthumous copy.

ENGLISH, mid-nineteenth-century
A bay horse, pony, bloodhound and dachshund, outside
Felbrigg Hall

FRANS VANDEVERDONCK (active *c.*1862–*c.*1889)
Ewe, lambs, and poultry in a landscape
Signed: *F. Vandeverdonck 1863*

LEFT OF WINDOW, OUTER COLUMN:

ALLAN DAVIDSON (1873–1932)
Emily Bayly, Mrs Wyndham Ketton-Cremer
(1882–1952)
Signed
The mother of Robert Wyndham Ketton-Cremer,
the last squire of Felbrigg, and wife of Wyndham
Ketton-Cremer (opposite).

FLEMISH, *c.*1600
Fantasy Landscape
In a fine Rococo frame of the kind made for the
Drawing Room and the Cabinet, so almost cer-
tainly acquired by William Windham II.

? GEORGE VINCENT (1796–1832)
River Scene
Bears signature: *GV 1825*
Inherited by R. W. Ketton-Cremer from two of his
Bayly aunts.

LEFT OF WINDOW, INNER COLUMN:

ANNA NISTRI, Signora TONELLI (*c.*1763–1846)
Unknown Young Man
Pastel. Oval. Inscribed on the back: *Anna Tonelli*
fece in Londra 1795

RIGHT OF WINDOW, INNER COLUMN:

ENGLISH, *c.*1830
Admiral Lukin (1768–1833)
Silhouette

N– M– (ENGLISH, *c.*1830)
Charles Ashe Windham (1810–70) as a subaltern
Wash drawing
For the sitter, see the Clint (right of window bay).

ENGLISH, early nineteenth-century
Felbrigg Cottage (formerly Parsonage)
Sepia wash
The two cannon on the lawn indicate that this was
probably executed when Admiral Lukin lived at the
Parsonage, between 1812 and 1824. It ceased to be
the Parsonage when the livings of Felbrigg and
Metton were combined in 1812, and has since been
demolished.

RIGHT OF WINDOW, OUTER COLUMN:

ALLAN DAVIDSON (1873–1932)
Wyndham Cremer Ketton-Cremer (1870–1933)
Wyndham Cremer Cremer, the son of Thomas
Wyndham Cremer and Rachel Ketton, added his
mother's surname to his own in 1924. Heir through
his mother to the Felbrigg estate, he was descended
through his father from the Orchard Wyndham line
of Wyndhams. Husband of Emily Bayly (opposite),
and father of the last squire of Felbrigg, Robert
Wyndham Ketton-Cremer.

E. W. GARRETT
The bombardment of Copenhagen, 1807
Grey wash, with touches of blue and red
William Lukin commanded the *Mars* during the
English assault with Congreve's Stick Rockets.

RIGHT OF WINDOW BAY:

GEORGE CLINT, ARA (1770–1854)
Captain Charles Ashe Windham (1810–70)
Second son of Admiral Lukin, and a captain in the
Coldstream Guards, he subsequently led the assault
on the Redan in the Crimean War (1855), and was
promoted to Major-General. It was he who pet-
itioned for the holding of the judicial enquiry, *De
Lunatico Inquirendo*, to certify his nephew William
Frederick Windham as a lunatic. Painted in 1833.

WILLIAM EDWARD WEST (1788–1857)
Cecilia Ann Windham, Mrs Henry Baring (1803–74)
Elder daughter of Admiral Lukin, and the second
wife of the third son of Sir Francis Baring, Bt.
Painted in 1833.

LEFT OF BAY WINDOW:

ENGLISH, *c.*1835
Henry Windham
An (illegitimate?) son of Admiral Lukin, and known
as 'Captain' Windham, though he only held a post
in the Coastguards.

RIGHT OF BAY WINDOW:

ENGLISH, *c.*1860
John Ketton (1808–72)
A Norwich merchant who had made a fortune out of oil-cake and cattle-feed in the 1830s and 1840s, and who acquired Felbrigg after 'Mad' Windham's bankers foreclosed on him in 1862.

LEFT OF DOOR, OUTER BAY:

ENGLISH, *c.*1870
Rachel Anna Ketton (1841–1932)
Daughter of John Ketton (alongside), married to Thomas Wyndham Cremer, to whose son Wyndham Cremer Cremer her childless brother made over Felbrigg in 1923.

CHARLES CATTON, RA (1728–98)
Thrower Buckle
Of Cringleford, Norfolk. His daughter Ann married Cremer (Woodrow) Cremer of Beeston Regis, Norfolk; and their son, the Rev. Cremer Cremer, married Marianne Wyndham.

LEFT OF DOOR, WITHIN BAY:

HENRY BERNARD CHALON (1771–1849)
'Rake', a white-and-tan spaniel
Coloured chalks. Signed and dated: *H. B. Chalon 1796*
Inscribed on the back by William Howe Windham: *Uncle Doughty's 'Rake'. He was offered £50 for him.*

J. HAWKSWORTH after J. S. COTMAN (1782–1842)
Felbrigg Hall from the south
Coloured engraving
Done for the *Excursions in the County of Norfolk* (1818–19). Cotman's wife, Ann Miles, was the daughter of a Felbrigg farmer.

– DALTON
George Thomas Wyndham (1806–30) and
Maria Augusta (Lukin) Windham (1805–71)
Silhouettes, inscribed as cut *8 March 1825*
George Thomas Wyndham was the brother of Marianne Wyndham, who married the Rev. Cremer Cremer. Maria Augusta, his wife, was the daughter of Admiral (Lukin) Windham, and after her first husband's death married the Earl of Listowel.

OVER DOOR:

ENGLISH, *c.*1850
William Frederick 'Mad' Windham (1840–66)
The penultimate Windham of Felbrigg, who inherited a heavily encumbered estate from his father,

and a rogue Hervey gene from his mother. Obsessed by playing with real trains, 'Mad Windham' fell prey to a *demi-mondaine*. His family failed to have him declared a lunatic, but the bank foreclosed. Felbrigg was bought by John Ketton and Windham ended as an 'Express' coach-driver.

FURNITURE

Fall-front, walnut veneer escritoire, *c.*1690, whose handles and feet were replaced *c.*1715 (possibly one bought by Katherine Windham in 1690/91).

Oval drop-leaf table with claw feet, *c.*1720.

Mahogany cheval fire-screen of *c.*1815 with contemporary needlework.

Fine burr yew veneer bureau of *c.*1720, possibly the 'large Ewe desk with book case & glass-doors' bought in 1735 by Ashe Windham for £8 16s from Elizabeth Gumley, who continued the business founded by her son John, a famous London carver, after his death in 1727.

Rosewood teapoy, *c.*1820.

Circular mahogany breakfast table with flame veneer top, *c.*1830s.

Oval drop-leaf table, *c.*1780, with well-preserved inlay of coloured woods.

Mahogany expanding dining-table, *c.*1830.

Dining-chairs, *c.*1830; maker's stamp: a leaf.

Mahogany double music stand and Canterbury of *c.*1800.

Glazed mahogany bureau-bookcase, late eighteenth-century.

BAROMETERS

Banjo barometer by Thompson of Yarmouth, *c.*1800.

French stick barometer incorporating thermometer by Tettamanzy of Rochefort, eighteenth-century.

CERAMICS

IN GLAZED BUREAU-BOOKCASE:

Service of Meissen plates and dishes painted with birds and flowers, *c.*1755–60.

CLOCK

Large late nineteenth-century eight-day clock in solid walnut case, reputedly made from timber grown on the estate. Dial made for three-train movement, now single-train, *c.*1920.

PIANO

Boudoir grand by Bechstein, *c.*1900.

THE GREAT HALL

The Great Hall of the Jacobean house, which had become by 1734 the 'common eating parlour', was entered through twin entrances in the old screen. In 1751 William Windham II made it into his neo-Tudor entrance hall with ten plaster busts on brackets and, by 1771, eighteen hall chairs (now in Screens Passage, Lobby and South Corridor), two tables and a longcase clock. By 1833 it had a large mahogany billiard table. The west bay window was blocked up by William Windham III in 1788 but opened again in 1842, when William Howe Windham recast the room in forceful neo-Jacobean pastiche with heavy oak doorcases and a new ceiling with huge wooden pendants. The architects were probably G. and J. C. Buckler, and at this stage it was painted a rich red. The present colour is postwar and introduced by R. W. Ketton-Cremer. Sir Brinsley Ford, who was his guest in 1953, recalls:

Although our visit took place in May it was still far too cold to inhabit the grand suite of rooms in the west wing, so we lived and had all our meals in the Great Hall. This was heated fairly effectively by a large and ugly anthracite stove round which we sat on the few chairs that were not piled high with books.

FIREPLACE

A Victorian design incorporating a beautiful armorial panel of the 1620s, celebrating ancient alliances. Left to right: Wyndham, Scrope, Tiptoft, Sydenham, Gambon, Wadham, Popham, Townshend, Wyndham. The stove is mid-twentieth-century, but the firedogs are *c.*1840.

STAINED GLASS

A collection amassed in the mid-nineteenth century by William Howe Windham.

FIRST WINDOW, TOP ROW:

Flemish roundels set in Victorian Gothic surrounds: 1 *The Sacrifice of Isaac, c.*1550; *The Charge to Peter*, seventeenth-century; an unidentified subject, *c.*1550; 2 *The Virgin and Child, c.*1525; *The Last Judgement, c.*1600; *The Resurrection, c.*1525; 3 an unidentified subject, *A king being presented with gifts, c.*1525; *St Matthew, c.*1600; an unidentified subject, *A conqueror reading edicts on a battlefield, c.*1525, in the style of Vellert.

LOWER ROW:

Copies by John Dixon of glass removed from St Peter Mancroft, Norwich, in 1837: 1 *The Visitation*; 2 *The Nativity*; 3 *The Adoration of the Magi*.

SECOND WINDOW, TOP ROW:

Three panels of glass *c.*1450 from St Peter Mancroft: 1 *Edmund Tudor, Earl of Richmond*; 2 *The Assumption of the Virgin*; 3 *St Anne and Cleophas*.

LOWER ROW:

Copies by Dixon: 1 *The Flight into Egypt*; 2 *The Massacre of the Innocents*; 3 *The Circumcision*.

SOUTH BAY, TOP ROW:

1 A sixteenth-century continental *female head* with a fragment of the *Windham arms*; 2 *Continental arms*, seventeenth-century; 3 Sixteenth-century *Continental arms* including those of *Andries Rademacher*, 1580; 4 Victorian panel of the *Windham Arms*; 5 Victorian panel with the *arms of Templetown*, the family of Lady Sophia Windham's mother; 6 *Continental arms* including those of *T. Miranda and Franses Lusitana*, 1690, and *William van Hamm*, 1645; 7 Flemish fragments including arms and a roundel of *The Prodigal Son Feasting, c.*1525–40; 8 Continental fragments and two roundels of unidentified subjects, upper *c.*1525–40, lower *c.*1600.

LOWER ROW:

Panels of continental glass set in Victorian diaper fields including an important group of Swiss panels: 1 *Collatinus finds Lucretia dying in the arms of her maid, c.*1525–40, in the style of pseudo-Ortkens; 2 *Fragment of an Angel*, French, sixteenth-century; 3 Victorian arms of *Sir Edmund Wyndham* (d.1569) in continental surround, *c.*1600, with Swiss panel of 1571 showing *Jacob Schwytzer and his wife Elsbett Lochmanin*, attributed to Fridly Burkhart and derived from two portraits by Tobias Stimmer in the Kunstmuseum, Basle; 4 Two Swiss panels: *Jörg Schwytzer*, 1571, attributed to Fridly Burkhart, and the arms of *Augustin Hofman, Abbot of Einseideln*, 1627; 5 Two Swiss panels: *The arms of the town of Lucerne, carried*

Cleophas and St Anne; stained glass panel, c.1450, from St Peter Mancroft, Norwich (second window, top row). Part of the collection amassed by William Howe Windham

by a knight, 1588, and a panel dedicated to *Adrien Burkhardt and Hans Bornhaus* with their arms and a scene illustrating *Matthew, chapter xxii*, c.1600, attributed to Wolfgang Spengler of Constance and originally from Weinfelden town hall; 6 Victorian arms, *Wyndham quartering Scrope and Tiptoft impaling Bacon*, set in a continental surround, and a Swiss panel of 1603 depicting the story of the dying *Scylurus and his sons*, and dedicated to *Caspar Melchior and Hans Jacob*; 7 French *angel*, sixteenth-century; 8 Fragment of a head and two Flemish roundels, *The Good Samaritan paying the Host*, c.1600, *Moses with the Tablets of the Law*, c.1600, with the arms of *Windham and Hervey*, Victorian.

WEST BAY, TOP ROW:

Glass from St Peter Mancroft: 1 Modern copy by Dennis King of *The Apostles Assembled* (original on display at St Peter's); 2 Dixon copy of *The Annunciation*; 3 Dixon copy of *The Nativity*; 4 *The Presentation in the Temple*, fifteenth-century; 5 *The Virgin foretells her Death*, fifteenth-century; 6 *St John tells the Apostles of the Virgin's Prophecy*, fifteenth-century.

LOWER ROW:

Six lights depicting *the arms of Windham and Hervey* set in continental surrounds within fields of Victorian patterns and inscriptions.

PICTURES

RIGHT OF DOOR:

Sir PETER LELY (1618–80) and Studio
Mary Ashe, Viscountess Townshend (1653–85)
The younger sister of Katherine Ashe, wife of William Windham I, painted soon after her marriage in 1673 to Horatio, 1st Viscount Townshend, but not at the same time or by the same artist as his portrait, though it is now framed and hung as its pendant.

ALLAN GWYNNE-JONES, RA (1892–1982)
Robert Wyndham Ketton-Cremer (1906–69)
Initialled and dated 1969–70
Biographer and Norfolk historian, the devoted preserver and recorder of Felbrigg, its last squire, and ultimately its donor to the National Trust. The portrait is unfinished, reputedly because the artist was reluctant to end the pretext for his agreeable visits to Felbrigg.

SOUTH-WEST CORNER:

GEORGE DANCE the Younger, RA, FRS, FSA (1741–1825)
Joseph Windham of Earsham, FSA (1739–1810)
Black chalk strengthened with brown ink
Signed, and inscribed with the identity of the sitter
Classical scholar and antiquary. He published only one work under his own name, but wrote significant contributions to the works of others, including Charles Cameron's *Baths of the Romans* (1772) and the second volume of James Stuart's *Antiquities of Athens* (1787 [1789]).

JOHN ADEY REPTON, FSA (1775–1860)
Oxnead Hall and its terraced garden
Brown ink and wash
The second seat of the Pastons, built by Admiral
Sir Clement Paston in the sixteenth century, and
pulled down by Admiral Lord Anson when he
bought the estate in the mid-eighteenth century.
This drawing is a sketch for an imaginary recon-
struction of it that was engraved by John Smith and
published in 1809. John Adey Repton was the
stone-deaf architect son of the architect and land-
scape-gardener Humphry Repton, and for a time he
lived in the remaining service wing of Oxnead. The
fountain was bought for Blickling in the Oxnead
sale of 1732, and placed in the centre of the parterre
in 1873.

LEFT OF WEST WINDOW:

Sir GODFREY KNELLER, Bt (1646/9–1723)
Portrait of an Unknown Lady with a whippet
(? Catherine Bowyer, Lady Ashe [1671 or after–1717])
This picture was painted around 1690, so it cannot,
as used to be thought, show Elizabeth Dobyns,
Mrs Ashe Windham, who was born only in 1693.
It may be the portrait of a mysterious '*Mrs Packer*'
listed in the Red Dressing Room in the 1771 inven-
tory; or, just possibly, of Catherine Bowyer, Lady
Ashe, a portrait of whom was also listed there. In

1698 the latter married Sir James Ashe, 2nd Bt
(1674–1733), who turned her out of the house for
refusing him his conjugal rights after his adultery.
In a fine Maratta frame *en suite* with the other
Windham portraits here.

RIGHT OF WEST WINDOW:

Manner of Sir PETER LELY (1618–80)
? Mary Wilson, Lady Ashe (c.1632–1705)
Traditionally called Catherine Bowyer (see above);
but since this was painted in the early 1670s, it
cannot be of her, and given that there is a copy of
it at Raynham inscribed 'L^y. Ash', it is much more
likely to show the wife of the 1st Bt, Sir Joseph
Ashe (Dining Room).

LEFT OF CHIMNEY-PIECE:

ANGLO-DUTCH, c.1640–50
Sir William Paston, 1st Bt (1610–62/3)
Son of Sir Edmund Paston (d.1632) of Paston and
Katherine Knyvett (d.1628/9) of Ashwellthorpe. In
1629 he moved into Oxnead Hall (see opposite
wall) with his new first wife, Lady Katherine Bertie,
and proceeded to embellish it with sculpture by
Nicholas Stone, collections of art and curiosity
(recorded by a singular picture in Norwich
Museum), and gardens descending to the River
Bure. After her death in 1636/7 he travelled to

*The Ketton sisters playing
billiards in the Great Hall
in the 1870s*

Jerusalem and Egypt, where he evidently experienced the adventure with the crocodile shown in the background, returning in 1639. Created baronet in 1641, he joined the Royalist cause, and was forced into exile in 1643–4 in Holland, where this picture might have been painted by Adriaen Hanneman (1601–71).

After RICHARD WILSON, RA (?1713–82)
Two figures by a ruin
Probably a copy of a lost painting by Wilson that was in the Ford collection, and which was etched by Thomas Hastings.

RIGHT OF CHIMNEY-PIECE:

Sir GODFREY KNELLER, Bt (1646/9–1723)
? *William Windham I* (1647–89)
Traditionally, but impossibly, called Sir James Ashe, 2nd Bt (1674–1733), this was painted by Kneller in the late 1680s – around the same time as his portrait of Ashe Windham (1673–1749) in the Dining Room – but clearly shows someone double the age of either of them then. Most probably, therefore, of Ashe's father, William Windham I, in his last years.

After THOMAS CRESWICK, RA (1811–69)
View of Cromer and its beach
Apparently copied from an engraving by Findon of Creswick's original painting; given to Ketton-Cremer by Guy Vaughan Morgan in 1951.

RIGHT OF DOOR TO STAIR HALL:

NORWICH SCHOOL, nineteenth-century
Windmill by moonlight
Acquired by Ketton-Cremer in 1936 as by Robert Ladbrooke (1769–1842).

LEFT OF DOOR FROM SCREENS PASSAGE:

Attributed to Sir RALPH COLE, Bt (1629–1704)
Horatio, 1st Viscount Townshend (1630–87)
William Windham I's neighbour at Raynham, fellow moderate supporter of the Country Party, and brother-in-law – having in 1673 married, as his second wife, Mary Ashe (see her portrait the other side of the door), the younger sister of Windham's wife, Katherine. The gentleman-painter Sir Ralph Cole's first wife was a Windham, of the Kentsford branch of the family.

After REMBRANDT (1606–69)
Portrait of an Unknown Woman
A copy of a picture of 1632 formerly in the Rothschild Collection in Paris. Recorded at Felbrigg in 1764, when it was thought to be a genuine picture by Rembrandt of his mother.

SCULPTURE

RIGHT OF DOOR TO SCREENS PASSAGE:

SEBASTIAN GAHAGAN (active 1800–35)
after JOSEPH NOLLEKENS, RA (1737–1823)
William Windham III (1750–1810)
Marble. Signed and dated 1821
A repetition of the posthumous bust on Windham's tomb in Felbrigg church. Gahagan was for many years Nollekens's assistant, but was miserably rewarded for it.

ON CHEST TO LEFT OF SOUTH WINDOW:

The Emperor Marcus Aurelius (ruled AD 161–180)
Equestrian bronze
After the Antique bronze on the Capitol in Rome, the plinth of which was designed by Michelangelo.

ON TABLE IN FRONT OF SOUTH WINDOW:

Three bronzes, all probably cast in the nineteenth century: *Flying Mercury* (after Giambologna, 1529–1608); the *Farnese Bull*, alias the *Fable of Dirce*, after a bronze reduction by Antonio Susini (active 1580–d.1624) of an Antique marble now in Naples. It tells the story of Dirce, second wife of King Lycus of Thebes, who was tied to a wild bull by her stepsons for her previous treatment of their mother; *Fortune balancing on a rudder*, after a ? Venetian bronze of the sixteenth century.

LEFT OF SOUTH BAY:

LORENZO BARTOLINI (1777–1850)
Frederick William Hervey, 1st Marquess of Bristol (1769–1859)
Marble
Father of William Howe Windham's wife, Lady Sophia Hervey. The pendant of his wife is at Ickworth in Suffolk.

ON TABLE BY DOOR TO STAIRCASE HALL:

Studio of ANTOINE-DENIS CHAUDET (1763–1810)
Colossal bust of Napoleon
Marble
William Windham III was an implacable opponent of Napoleon, and devoted a lot of energy to training a volunteer corps against invasion via Norfolk.

RIGHT OF SOUTH BAY:

Sir FRANCIS CHANTREY, RA (1781–1841)
Arthur Wellesley, 1st Duke of Wellington
(1769–1852)
Marble
Chantrey was a regular guest at Holkham, nearby.

IN WEST WINDOW BAY:

Two marble busts from the studio of, or after, JOSEPH NOLLEKENS, RA (1737–1823) of *Charles James Fox* (1749–1806) and *William Pitt the Younger* (1759–1806). All these 'political' busts were collected by William Howe Windham, and placed here on scagliola half-columns *c.*1840.

IN WEST WINDOW BAY:

Laocoön
Bronze
A nineteenth-century cast after the celebrated Antique marble rediscovered in Rome in 1506. It shows the Trojan priest Laocoön and his two sons, crushed by snakes sent by the goddess Athene for their impiety in doubting (rightly) that the wooden horse left by the Greeks was really a votive offering.

LEFT OF DOOR FROM SCREENS PASSAGE:

ANGELO BIENAIMÉ (active 1829–51)
Sir Robert Peel, Bt (1788–1850)
Marble
The great Tory Prime Minister, carved around 1840, as the culminating figure in this gallery of political busts.

FURNITURE

ON EITHER SIDE OF ENTRANCE DOOR:

Two marble-topped oak side-tables of *c.*1840.

ON SOUTH WALL AND IN BAY:

Walnut chairs of two different but related patterns (makers' stamps 'I.M.' and 'H'), possibly intended for William Windham II's dining-room of 1751 (see p.25).
Oyster veneer walnut cabinet of *c.*1720, possibly 'A walnut tree cabinet of Gumleys' bought by Ashe Windham for £10 in 1735.
Miniature mahogany kneehole desk, *c.*1730.
Small eighteenth-century mahogany hanging bookcase containing R. W. Ketton-Cremer's personal copies of his own publications.

IN SOUTH BAY:

Rococo mahogany table with marble slab, labelled 'N13 for Wm Windham Esq Felbrigg near Cromer Norfolk', 1750s.

ON WEST WALL AND IN WEST BAY:

Mahogany bureau bookcase, *c.*1780.
Heavily carved knee-hole desk, *c.*1840.
A walnut armchair with solid, shaped back, *c.*1730.
Walnut bookcase with glazed doors, *c.*1730.
Tall, seven-fold, Chinese Coromandel lacquer screen, *c.*1700.
Two upholstered mahogany camel-back sofas from the 1750s Drawing Room furniture, re-covered to match the modern armchairs.
Heavily carved octagonal oak centre table, *c.*1840.

CERAMICS

French oval blue-and-white faience cistern painted in the Chinese manner, *c.*1700.
Lowestoft blue-and-white mug.

CARPET

Savonnerie design of 1851, made for the Great Exhibition.

WAX PORTRAIT

IN OVAL FRAME BELOW HANGING BOOKCASE:

George II, attributed to Isaac Gosset.

THE DINING ROOM

The deep doorway between the two rooms connects the Jacobean house with the west wing that was built by William Windham I in the 1680s and brings us into the series of rooms wonderfully transformed by his grandson William Windham II. This room was formed by James Paine in 1752 out of the space previously occupied by the 1680s staircase. It is closely related to the contemporary schemes for two adjacent rooms – the lost interior of the Great Hall and that of the present Stair Hall. The plasterwork was undertaken by Joseph Rose the elder, with the assistance of George Green.

Hung with portraits of Windham's parents and grandparents, its oval mirrors (four with bevelled

*The Dining
Room*

edges were salvaged from a 1680s room) ornamented with lead chains alluding to the Windhams'
fetterlock badge, it has been described as 'a Rococo
evocation of a Caroline room'. The pale lilac is
thought to be the original colour (see p.26), but the
dado was originally off-white and the doors were
grained to resemble a dark wood (like the doors on
the stairs) and would have augmented the sombre
grandeur of the old portraits. The room was redecorated by Mr Dixon of Norwich in 1824; the
detailed painter's bill covers plaster mouldings,
doors, dadoes and window surrounds but not the
walls themselves.

CEILING

In April 1752 Windham had 'chose 4 casts of the
seasons for the corners of the ceiling of the new
eating parlour'. These, with the symbols of the
chase above the doors, are typical dining-room
imagery. The division into framed fields imitates
the 1680s ceilings, for instance in the Drawing
Room.

FIREPLACE

Windham ordered a marble fireplace from William
Biggs of Bath in 1751 but angrily cancelled the
order when progress was delayed and had the plasterers execute Paine's design in hard stucco (see
p.25). The grapes and vine leaves are often found
in dining-rooms. The grate is mid-nineteenth-
century but the fire-irons *c*.1830.

PICTURES

OVER MANTELPIECE:

Sir PETER LELY (1618–80) and Studio
Sir Joseph Ashe, 1st Bt (1618–86)
His two eldest daughters, Katherine (1652–1729)
and Mary (1653–85), married William Windham I
and Horatio, 1st Viscount Townshend, respectively.
He was a wealthy merchant trading with Flanders,
whose financial aid to the Royalist cause earned him
a baronetcy at the Restoration. He put together a
large estate in Twickenham, later named, after a
subsequent owner, Cambridge Park.

LEFT OF DOOR FROM GREAT HALL:

Attributed to THOMAS BARDWELL (1703/4–67)
? Elizabeth Dobyns, Mrs Windham (1693–1736)
Ashe Windham married Elizabeth Dobyns in 1709, on the rebound from the death of Hester Buckworth (see Stair Hall). They were soon at odds, and after the belated birth in 1717 of their only child, William II, lived apart. This is the only portrait now at Felbrigg that could be of her, though the costume seems to postdate her death. Perhaps, therefore, a posthumous commission, from William Windham II after the death of his father in 1749, so as to have both parents represented in the classic room for portraits in the house.

OVERDOOR:

Sir GODFREY KNELLER, Bt (1646/9–1723)
Col. William Windham, MP (1674–1730),
of Earsham
Oval. Signed with monogram
Younger brother of Ashe Windham, who – as the eldest son who had already inherited Felbrigg – was painted by Kneller in larger format (alongside). This may be the portrait for which their mother paid Kneller £15 in 1696. He lost a leg at the Battle of Blenheim (1704), but continued to campaign in the rest of the War of the Spanish Succession. In 1705 he married Anne, daughter of Sir Charles Tyrrell of Heron Manor, Essex, and at first lived in Braxted in the same county, along with his mother. Unlike her, he came well out of the South Sea

Bubble, and was able in 1721 to buy Earsham. Recorded here in 1764 and 1771.

RIGHT OF DOOR TO GREAT HALL:

Sir GODFREY KNELLER, Bt (1646/9–1723)
Ashe Windham, MP (1673–1749)
Possibly painted in the lifetime of his father, William Windham I (see the following, but especially the portrait of him in the Great Hall), and definitely before he embarked on the Grand Tour, 1693–6. At Felbrigg he built the Orangery and the service courtyard in its early form, and probably bought much of the early eighteenth-century furniture which remains in the house. Almost certainly the picture recorded here in 1764 and 1771, along with a pendant of his wife.

LEFT OF DOOR TO DRAWING ROOM:

Sir PETER LELY (1618–80)
William Windham I (1647–89)
Probably painted by Lely before the sitter's marriage in 1669, and given by his widow, along with her own portrait (on the other side of the door), to their son Ashe, on his marriage in 1709. Eldest surviving son of Thomas Windham's second marriage, to Elizabeth Mede, William I inherited from his half-brother, John, in 1665. Although his neighbour, Sir John Hobart, tried to persuade him to stand as MP, William I preferred 'ease at home, love of privacy, and good husbandry'. He got the gentleman-amateur architect William Samwell to

*Paine's design for
the north wall of the
Dining Room*

design a new west wing for the house (1674–87), and planted quantities of trees on the estate, particularly chestnuts.

OVERDOOR TO DRAWING ROOM:

Attributed to ENOCH SEEMAN (c.1694–1745)
Capt. Charles Windham (d.1747)
Younger son of Col. William Windham of Earsham (whose portrait is opposite), and nephew of Ashe Windham and of James Windham, with whom he first went to sea in the *Diamond* in 1723, to harry the pirates in the Caribbean. His most distinguished action was, when captain of the *Rose*, the burning of two 'Sallee Rovers', or Barbary Pirates, in Mogador Bay in May 1734 (see the picture by Paton in the Drawing Room).

RIGHT OF DOOR TO DRAWING ROOM:

Sir PETER LELY (1618–80) and Studio
Katherine Ashe, Mrs William Windham (1652–1729)
The eldest daughter of Sir Joseph Ashe (whose portrait by Lely is over the chimney-piece) and sister of Mary Ashe, Viscountess Townshend (whose portrait by Lely is in the Drawing Room). A devoted wife, mother and grandmother, in her letters she gives a vivid picture of her management of Felbrigg and of her family. Lely took the pose from a portrait of Mary of Modena he had painted shortly after her marriage to James (II), Duke of York in 1673 (Ranger's House, Blackheath), just changing the face.

SCULPTURE

ON MANTELPIECE (LEFT TO RIGHT):

Three nineteenth-century Italian bronze reductions of *Silenus holding the Infant Bacchus*, *The Dying Gladiator* or *Gaul*, and *Young Faun carrying a kid over his shoulders*.

LEFT AND RIGHT, ABOVE:

A pair of bronzed plaster busts of *Homer* and *Sappho*, supplied by John Cheere in 1752.

FURNITURE

Mahogany Sheraton sofa-table with satinwood banding and ebony handles, c.1800.

Mahogany dining-chairs with leather seats and backs (faded now but once green), stamped 'L.' and 'J.S.', c.1830, and a pair of mahogany fireside chairs to match.

Hepplewhite mahogany dining-table, c.1790.

Pair of carved mahogany serving-tables, c.1750. These are mentioned in the 1771 inventory but the survivors of the '19 Walnut Tree Chairs With Leather Bottoms' are probably the simple eighteenth-century chairs now in the Great Hall and the corridors. Slight differences may be explained by William Windham's letter of 31 March 1752: 'Pray likewise send a drawing of the back of one of the leather chairs which are in the great parlour. We want to know to make more by.'

Brass-bound mahogany cellaret and wine pail, c.1800.

Mahogany cluster-column pole-screen with contemporary needlepoint panel, c.1760.

Mahogany sofa-table with pillar legs, c.1800.

CERAMICS AND GLASS

Coalport and Ridgway dessert services, mid-nineteenth-century. Glass of the same period and earlier.

CARPET

Axminster, c.1900.

THE DRAWING ROOM

Known until the nineteenth century as the 'Great Parlour', this was the main reception and dining-room of the Caroline house, panelled in oak and hung with pictures. A fragment of its parquetry floor may be seen on the threshold. It was remodelled by James Paine in 1751, retaining the original ceiling. Paine's doorcases and richly moulded dado respond to its magnificent plasterwork with spirited carving of his own time. William Windham II conceived it as a room to display the cream of his Grand Tour purchases. His marine pictures still dominate the room but we have to try to imagine the fireplace wall in 1771 with 'Mr Dagnia painted by Shackleton' (see p.65) as the overmantel, flanked by 'An Old Usurer Rembrant' (see p.64) and 'Sir William Paston of the Yarmouth Family' (see p.46).

CEILING

Dated in Roman numerals 1687, this is one of the finest ceilings of its period, identical in its craftsmanship to an exactly contemporary one at Melton Constable Hall. Both are probably by Edward

The Drawing Room

Goudge, who undertook very similar work at Belton in Lincolnshire in 1688–9. The wonderfully modelled local game birds in the corner compartments, which include pheasants, partridges, mallard, woodcocks and plovers, would have especially pleased the patron William Windham I (whose fetterlock badge may be seen near the north-west corner), as would the sprays of oak and pine cones. But there are also magnificent fruits and flowers, among them pears, grapes, quinces, apricots, lemons, almonds, pea-pods, pomegranates, roses, orange flowers and sea shells. This imagery of feasting reflects the room's original purpose. A drawing annotated in William Windham III's hand, which shows the plain areas of the ceiling tinted in pale orange, probably dates from around 1788, when the

Norwich plasterers Cato and Swain were paid for the new cornice, which is much shallower than its Caroline predecessor.

FIREPLACE

The 1680s chimney-piece from this room is now in the Library. Its white and Siena marble successor of 1751, probably by Thomas Carter, was tried first in the Cabinet by William Windham II before finding its place here. The polished steel and brass grate is of *c*.1830.

DECORATION

In 1771 the room had a flowered red paper. It was hung with the present damask by Admiral Windham *c*.1830, when the windows were given the '3 pr of splendid window curtains, crimson damask furniture with gilt cornices, pins, drapery and holland covers'; in 1863 these and the other furnishings were protected by 'Three outside Venetian blinds'.

PICTURES

OVER CHIMNEY-PIECE:

JOHN JACKSON, RA (1778–1831) after
Sir THOMAS LAWRENCE, PRA (1769–1830)
William Windham III (1750–1810)
The last of the true Windhams of Felbrigg, its only owner to perform upon the national stage, diarist, and friend of Samuel Johnson. Irresolute for many years over his entry upon both public life and matrimony, he began to play an active part in politics as one of the Whigs who came to support the war with France, serving as belligerent Secretary at War in Pitt's Cabinet from 1794 to 1801. In 1798 he finally married Cecilia Forrest, after a long-standing platonic affair with her sister Bridget. Resigning with Pitt in 1801, he was Secretary for War and the Colonies in Grenville's 'Ministry of all the Talents' in 1806–7. Known to his opponents as 'Weathercock Windham' for his oscillation between Fox and Pitt, he saw himself as 'a scholar among politicians and a politician among scholars'. The original of this portrait was exhibited by Lawrence at the RA in 1803, and is at the sitter's college (University College, Oxford).

LEFT AND RIGHT OF CHIMNEY-PIECE:

? GERMAN, mid-eighteenth-century
A pair of studies of Pandour Horsemen
Almost certainly picked up by William Windham II on his travels, which may have taken him to eastern Europe. The Pandours were ferocious irregulars from Croatia, who were formed into a corps to defend the throne of the Empress Maria Theresa in 1741. Reminiscent of a German artist such as August Querfurt (1696–1761).

RIGHT OF CHIMNEY-PIECE (BOTTOM TO TOP):

After BARTOLOMÉ ESTEBAN MURILLO (1618–82)
The Infant John the Baptist
A copy of the painting in the National Gallery.

The Battle of the Texel (1673); by Willem van de Velde the Elder and Younger (Drawing Room)

? ENGLISH, mid-eighteenth-century
A young woman at a window in ? Balkan costume
The turban, plume and generally exotic dress suggest someone from eastern Europe; the fur trimmings further point to an inhabitant of high mountain country – possibly Albania? Another indication that William Windham II may have visited eastern Europe.

OVER DOOR TO RIGHT OF CHIMNEY-PIECE:

Manner of FRANCESCO ZUCCARELLI (1702–88)
Herd-folk by a stream
Probably one of the pair of pictures listed in this room in 1764 as simply a 'Landskip by Zaccarelli', although it is actually the work of an imitator.

LEFT OF DOOR TO DINING ROOM (BOTTOM TO TOP):

WILLEM VAN DE VELDE the Elder (1611–93) and WILLIAM VAN DE VELDE the Younger (1633–1707)
The Battle of the Texel (1673): the bombardment of the Royal Prince
The Battle of the Texel was the last major seafight of the three Anglo-Dutch wars, in which the Dutch admiral, De Ruyter, thwarted the English commander-in-chief Prince Rupert's attempt to draw out and destroy his fleet, in order to make way for a joint invasion of Holland with the French. This picture shows the crucial episode of the battle, when Cornelis Tromp's flagship, the *Gouden Leeuw* (*Golden Lion*), bombarded the flagship of Admiral Sir Edward Spragge so severely that the latter was forced to abandon it.

Of the two Van de Veldes, the father was most celebrated as an eye-witness recorder of the actions of the Dutch and English navies, but this was the one engagement at which he was not present. The son was much the finer painter and more skilled at creating compositions featuring every kind of ship; he had the greater hand in this one of the great pair of scenes showing the battle that were later acquired by William Windham II. In 1934 Ketton-Cremer was forced to sell this picture – his one and only major disposal – in order to pay for essential repairs. It has now been kindly lent back to the house by the National Maritime Museum, to which he had sold it.

After, or Studio of, CLAUDE-JOSEPH VERNET (1714–89)
Italian Harbour Scene on a Misty Morning
Vernet worked in Rome from 1734 to 1753, and it is possible that William Windham II acquired it there. Recorded in this place in 1764.

OVER DOOR TO DINING ROOM:

RICHARD PATON (1717–91)
The destruction of two Sallee rovers by the Rose *and the* Shoreham *in Mogador Bay (1734)*
Sallee was a notorious nest of pirates upon the Barbary (ie Moroccan) coast. William Windham II hung this picture in a similar position in the Cabinet.

RIGHT OF DOOR TO DINING ROOM (BOTTOM TO TOP):

WILLEM VAN DE VELDE the Elder (1611–93)
The Battle of the Texel (1673): the engagement of the two fleets
The pendant to the picture on the other side of the door, but unlike it, entirely by Van de Velde the father, painted not long after the event. It shows a somewhat later moment, just before Spragge transferred his flag from the *Royal Prince* (in the left foreground, with only her foremast standing) to the *St George* (at the left with a blue flag at the main); close to starboard of the *Prince* is the *Gouden Leeuw*.

Studio of WILLIAM VAN DE VELDE the Younger (1633–1707)
A Kaag and a smalschip before a strong breeze
Fishing pinks with an approaching storm
The marines at Felbrigg were almost all collected by William Windham II, who, according to a fellow-member of the Genevan 'Common Room', Richard Aldworth, 'could and did build vessels, and navigate them himself'. Hence, perhaps, his preference for scenes that showed ships at grips with strong winds, over the calms for which Van de Velde the Younger was more celebrated.

LEFT OF DOOR TO CABINET (BOTTOM TO TOP):

SAMUEL SCOTT (?1702–72)
Old London Bridge
Scott painted this motif no fewer than eleven times, first in 1747, the year after the Lord Mayor had called a Court of Enquiry to consider the future of the bridge, which was a dangerous obstacle to traffic on the Thames. The houses on it were pulled down, and a single central arch built, in 1757, but the rest of the bridge was not demolished until 1831. The

Old London Bridge; by Samuel Scott (Drawing Room)

1764 inventory records that this version was painted in 1753, which is also the year in which William Windham II requested frames for it and its pendant.

Studio of WILLIAM VAN DE VELDE the Younger (1633–1707)
A Dutch flagship running before a gale
See above.

OVER DOOR TO CABINET:

? RANELAGH BARRETT or BARWICK (active c.1737–d.1768) after ? ABRAHAM STORCK (1644–1708/10)
A state barge and other shipping near the shore
Probably one of the pictures introduced by Admiral Lukin. The attribution is based on an old inscription formerly on the back of the frame. Barrett/Barwick was a very celebrated copyist – albeit primarily of portraits by Rubens, Van Dyck and Kneller.

RIGHT OF DOOR (BOTTOM TO TOP):

SAMUEL SCOTT (?1702–72)
The Thames by the Tower of London
Scott painted this motif only slightly fewer times than its pendant here, the first version dating from 1746. The three pairs of 'S' braces on the chimney

at the right may be a concealed signature. The prominent vessel in the foreground is a Danish timber vessel, known as a 'cat bark'.

Studio of WILLIAM VAN DE VELDE the Younger (1633–1707)
A smalschip before an approaching storm
See above.

OVER DOOR TO LEFT OF CHIMNEY-PIECE:

Manner of JEAN-BAPTISTE LALLEMAND (1716–1803)
Evening Landscape with an estuary and ruined temple
Four 'Landskips by Allemand' were recorded on this wall of the Drawing Room in 1764 and 1771. This picture and a now wanting pendant, both in the manner of Lallemand, were probably two of them, and the others the Julliars now in the West Corridor.

LEFT OF CHIMNEY-PIECE:

WILLEM VAN HERP (1614–77)
Achilles discovered amongst the daughters of Lycomedes
In an attempt to prevent Achilles going off to fight and meet his death in the Trojan war, his mother Thetis sent him to finish his education, disguised as a girl, at the court of Lycomedes, King of Scyros. The Greeks, knowing that they could not take Troy without his aid, sent Ulysses to find him. This he

did by pretending to be a merchant with jewels to sell; but amongst these were arms, which Achilles' manly nature drove him to try on instead of the trinkets, thus revealing himself. Van Herp was a later imitator of Rubens, working on a smaller scale.

Sir JOSHUA REYNOLDS, PRA (1723–92)
George Cholmondeley (1752–1830)
One of the very last portraits to have been painted by Reynolds, and remarkable as a foretaste of similar portraits by Hoppner and Lawrence, it was shown at the RA in 1790 and much praised. It was painted for William Windham III, in exchange for a portrait of Windham by Reynolds (now in the National Portrait Gallery). Cholmondeley was his closest friend, and Windham at one point made a will leaving Felbrigg to him and then to Cholmondeley's eldest son by his mistress, Cecilia Forrest, whom Windham was ultimately himself to marry.

PHILIPPE MERCIER (1689/91–1760)
A Young Woman with Roses: 'Spring'
Monogrammed
Engraved by R. Purcell after 1755 as one of a set of the four *Seasons*.

FURNITURE

In 1771 its movable furniture consisted of '2 Large Settees, Covered with Crimson Damask, with Bolsters, 14 Mahogany chairs, With Crimson Damask Bottoms and Red and White Check Covers to the Setees and Chairs, a Very fine India Screen, With Six Leaves' and 'a Very Large Turkey Carpet' (the chairs and sofas are now in the Stone Corridor, West Corridor and Great Hall).

The following pieces, mostly still in the room, were added by Admiral Windham and are thus described in the 1833 inventory:

12 splendid gilt chairs with Crimson Damask furniture and chintz covers [maker's stamp 'J.S.', like those in the Dining Room].

2 fire screens to match.

2 elbow and one easy chair to match.

Sofa, squab and four pillows to match.

Four antique elbow chairs and covers [from a 1750s bedroom and now in the Cabinet].

2 splendid gilt brackets [1750s, from the Cabinet].

2 pier glasses.

3 holland blinds.

2 imitation marble brackets [i.e. the pier-tables re-

placing the eighteenth-century ones which had white marble tops in 1771].

Pair of Rosewood card tables and covers [in the window reveals at either end].

Rosewood centre table and cover.

All the new pieces were of *c*.1830 and most appear to have been supplied by William Freeman of Norwich.

In addition to those listed above:

A Boulle *bureau Mazarin*, later nineteenth-century.

Chandelier given to R.W. Ketton-Cremer by Miss Robinson of Knapton Hall *c*.1967.

A Boulle writing table, nineteenth-century (possibly one described in 1833).

Two small chests in solid mahogany with a lighter veneer and elaborate brass hinges, Hispanic, nineteenth-century.

A small Boulle table with cabriole legs (possibly one described in 1833), early nineteenth-century.

Giltwood fire-screen with needlework panel, mid-nineteenth-century.

Inlaid gaming table with gilt ornaments in the French style, nineteenth-century.

CARPET

An 'English Savonnerie' design of *c*.1851.

METALWORK

ON CHIMNEY-BREAST:

Ormolu Rococo candle branches, *c*.1750 (from the Cabinet).

ON BOULLE TABLES:

Four Rococo ormolu candlesticks, probably eighteenth-century.

CERAMICS

New Hall teapot given by Queen Mary.

Series of Meissen dishes painted with flowers, *c*.1755–60.

Pair of large mid-nineteenth-century Chinese *famille rose* hexagonal vases.

ON CHIMNEY-PIECE:

Pair of French late eighteenth-century biscuit figure groups, signed 'Constant'.

Pair of early Meissen square bottles in the Kakiemon style, *c*.1725.

CLOCK

Bracket clock in ebonised case by Thomas Tompion, *c*.1690 (on loan to Felbrigg).

SCULPTURE

Small marble bust of the *Duke of Wellington*, mid-nineteenth-century.

THE CABINET

This was built as the 'Drawing Room' of the 1680s wing (the room to which family and guests would withdraw after meals in the adjacent Great Parlour). It was square in plan and panelled until the bay window was added in 1751, when William Windham II remodelled the room as the setting for the Italian pictures which he had acquired on the Grand Tour. The recast room with its new dadoes and doorcase was sufficiently advanced for its decoration to be discussed with Paine in December 1751, and in the following January Windham requested drawings of its walls and those of the Great Parlour so that he could plan the picture hang.

CEILING

The square plaster ceiling of *c*.1687 survives; its plan is similar to that over the staircase at Belton, which Edward Goudge was to execute in 1688–9. The Rococo filling of the central panel, the delicately modelled cove with its trails of flowers and the arms of Windham and his wife Sarah Hicks (see p.25), and the ceiling of the bay were designed by Paine and represent two months' work by George Green with the assistance of John Wegg, commencing in October 1750 and ending in January 1751, when twelve pounds of glovers' shreds were bought to size the whitewash for it. Cato and Swaine's bill for '90 feet of Enrich'd Cornice in Bow Drawing Room' of 1788 may refer to the dentil cornice.

FIREPLACE

This has a complex history. The marble surround and the polished steel grate are of 1789, when the Norwich mason John Blackburn was paid £42 for 'a New Marble Chimney Piece in the Bow Room Parlour'. The richly carved central plaque was supplied by a London carver. This ensemble replaced a chimney-piece supplied in July 1752 by Thomas Carter which appears to have been decorated with flowers. This was itself commissioned as a substitute for the chimney-piece in the present Drawing Room, which William Windham II had intended originally for the Cabinet.

DECORATION

The hangings and the gilded cord edging had been ordered in 1751. The crimson worsted damask is remarkably well preserved and the size of its single repeat, which runs very nearly from cornice to chair rail, is unusual. The gilt cornice and pelmet over the window belong to curtains introduced by Admiral Windham *c*.1830.

PICTURES

The Cabinet has long been celebrated as the epitome of the Grand Tour, an almost unique, virtually intact survival of an eighteenth-century collection made on such a tour, hung as the collector himself planned it, the very drawings for which, drawn up to Windham's instructions by Paine's foreman, Hull, and annotated by him, still exist in the archive.

The hang was conceived in tandem with that of the Drawing Room, as the matching character of the different Rococo patterns of the frames (probably by René Duffour) in the two rooms indicate. It was carried out in 1752–3, with Windham himself present, as he had insisted to his steward, Frary. In the Drawing Room, marines and naval engagements set the tone, but landscape and topography complement these; in the Cabinet, the proportions are reversed, and, amongst the landscapes, a very special place is given to six large oils and 26 little gouaches of Rome and its environs by Giovanni Battista Busiri, known as 'Titarella' (1698–1757), for which Windham evidently had an especial predilection, and that he had acquired or ordered when in Rome in 1739 (they are variously dated 1739 or 1740).

Many of the gouaches are of classic sites, but with a preference for bridges, tombs and other Antique ruins standing in nature, for Windham evidently had a particular fondness for the Roman Campagna itself. The titles (and orthography) used here are found on the back of them; where one is lacking, the suggested title is put within square brackets.

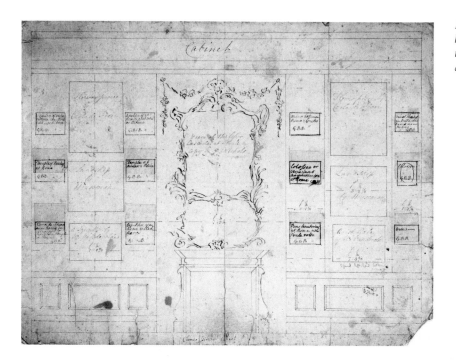

FROM OVERMANTEL, CLOCKWISE, BOTTOM TO TOP

(*Refer to picture diagrams*):

1 JOSEPH NICKOLLS (active 1726–55), after G. B. BUSIRI (1698–1757)
The Grand Cascade at Tivoli
A copy of no.10. Windham evidently failed to think of an overmantel when commissioning his six oils from Busiri, and he must have been reluctant to cut into either of the uprights amongst them to make one. Instead he went to a London view-painter for this enlarged copy of what was perhaps the most celebrated and often-painted view in Italy.

RIGHT OF CHIMNEY-PIECE, LEFT OF DOOR:

2–4 G. B. BUSIRI, three gouaches (bottom to top):
Pons Senatorius now called Ponte Rotto; Amphitheatre of Vespasian at Rome called Colosseo; View between Rome and Loretto

ON DOOR:

5 JAN BAPTIST HUYSMANS (1654–1716)
A mountainous landscape with women fetching water
Although this picture and its pendant (no.45) are by a Flemish artist, his conception of both landscape and figures is entirely idealised and classicising. As

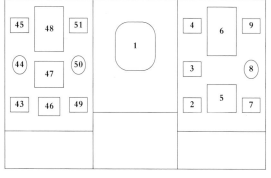

EAST WALL

Windham planned it, '*A Squall*' by Van de Velde hung on the door, but has had to be removed for safety to the Yellow Bedroom.

6 KAREL VAN VOGELAER, called CARLO DEI FIORI (1653–95)
Flowerpiece
For this room Windham acquired a pair of flower-pieces, not by some ordinary Dutch artist, or by the inevitable Monnoyer or Bogdany, but by a Flemish artist working in Rome – which was no doubt where he acquired them.

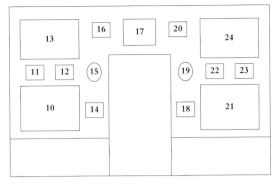

SOUTH WALL

RIGHT OF DOOR:

7–9 G. B. BUSIRI, three gouaches (bottom to top):
[? *A grotto near Naples*]; *Vespasian's Amphitheatre now called Colosseo at Rome*; *View of the Theatre made in the garden of the Villa Madama near Rome for the first acting of the 'Pastor Fido'*

10–13 G. B. BUSIRI, two oils and two gouaches (from bottom to top):
[*The Grand Cascade at Tivoli*]; *Sepulchre of Plautius near Tivoli & the Ponte Lucano* (on left); *Ponte Salario, an antique bridge near Rome* (on right); [*Prospect of Frascati*]

IMMEDIATELY TO LEFT OF DOOR:

14–16 G. B. BUSIRI, three gouaches (bottom to top):
Fountain near Marino, a village near Rome; *Cascade of Tivoli of the Anio of Teverone*; *Ponte Maniolo, a Roman Antique bridge near Rome*

OVER DOOR:

17 CORNELIS VAN POELENBURGH (c.1594/5–1667)
Nymphs bathing by ruins
Not recorded in the 1764 or 1771 inventories, despite being in a frame of the kind made for pictures in the Cabinet and Drawing Room, so it is possible that it has taken the place – and the frame – of a Berchem recorded then, but not since. Both Poelenburgh and Berchem painted Italianate and idealised landscapes.

IMMEDIATELY TO RIGHT OF DOOR:

18–20 G. B. BUSIRI, three gouaches (bottom to top):
A Bridge near Tivoli called Ponte del'Aqua Auria; *View of the fall of the Velino near Terni*; *View on the road between Rome and Loretto*

FAR RIGHT OF DOOR TO DRAWING ROOM:

21–4 G. B. BUSIRI, two oils and two gouaches (from bottom to top):
[*The Cascatelle at Tivoli*]; *View on the road between Rome and Loretto* (left); *Ponte Nomentano, an antique bridge near Rome* (right); [*The Aqueduct at Civita Castellana*]

LEFT OF SEAFIGHT (BOTTOM TO TOP):

25 JOHANNES GLAUBER (1646–c.1726)
Greek Maidens venerating a statue of Pan amongst tombs
Signed: *GLAUBER*
Glauber was a Netherlandish artist who produced classicising landscapes, after spending four years in Italy, where Windham may have acquired this picture and its pendant (no.31).

26 G. B. BUSIRI
[*Capriccio of a waterfall with the tomb of Cecilia Metella*]
The exception to the actual – if embellished – views of classical sites that Windham seems to have preferred to commission from Busiri.

WALL OPPOSITE CHIMNEY-PIECE, CENTRE:

27 SIMON DE VLIEGER (c.1600–53)
A Battle between Dutch ships and Chinese junks
Signed: *S. DE VLIEGER 1650*
Recently identified as showing the destruction of

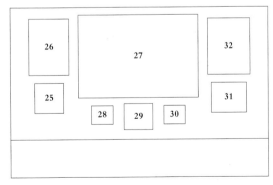

WEST WALL

Chinese junks at Amoy on 13 July 1633, on the strength of the fact that the flagship (on the right) is inscribed as the *Texel*. However, the other two named ships, the *Domburch* and the *Arnemude*, did not take part on this Pearl-Harbor-type attack on the unprepared Chinese fleet, which makes this interpretation doubtful.

BELOW (LEFT TO RIGHT):

28 ABRAHAM STORCK (*c.*1635–after 1704)
Capriccio of the Grand Harbour, Valletta
Signed: *A. Storck. Fecit. 1673*
One of three little paintings by Storck added to the collection by Admiral Windham. Nos 28 and 30 and the Bakhuysen (no.29) are already shown here in a hanging-plan of 1835, having displaced two of the Busiris and the Wouwerman to the window wall. Storck seems never to have visited Malta, and this capriccio appears to have been based on a drawing made in 1664 by a fellow Amsterdam artist, Willem Schellincks (*c.*1627–78), for the topographical collections of Laurens van der Hem.

29 LUDOLF BAKHUYSEN (1631–1708)
Dutch shipping in choppy seas
Initialled on foreground buoy: *LB*
An inscription on the back of this picture, *Admiral Lukin, Poste Namur*, seems to indicate that it was acquired by the retired vice-admiral when he was living in Brussels in 1820–21.

30 ABRAHAM STORCK (*c.*1635–after 1704)
Capriccio of Leghorn
Signed: *A. Storck Fecit*
Leghorn (Livorno) was the seaport of Tuscany, noted for its galleys (one of which is seen in this picture) manned by convicts.

RIGHT OF SEAFIGHT (BOTTOM TO TOP):

31 JOHANNES GLAUBER (1646–*c.*1726)
Classical landscape with the Nymphs of Diana resting from the chase
Signed: *GLAUBER*
The works of Glauber and his younger brother, Jan Gottlieb (1656–1704), who accompanied him to Italy, have never been properly distinguished, and the undifferentiated signature on nos 25 and 31 could suggest a collaboration between them.

32 G. B. BUSIRI
[*The Falls of the Velino at Terni*]
The Falls at Terni were the next most celebrated in Italy to those of Tivoli.

RETURN WALL, LEFT OF WINDOW BAY:

33, 34 G. B. BUSIRI, pair of gouaches (bottom to top):
Ruin near Rome called Torre ai Schiavi, supposed to have been a Temple of Peace or Quiet; Cascade of Tivoli seen from underneath the bridge [*the Ponte San Rocco*]

35 After PHILIPS WOUWERMAN (1619–68)
Men loading a boat at Scheveningen
Scheveningen is the seaport of The Hague. The initials *PW* were once found on this picture, and could have been an attempt to pass this later variant copy of a popular Wouwerman off as an original. On Windham's hanging-plan it appears under the middle of no.27.

36 PIETRO BIANCHI (1694–1740)
Sepulchre of [*Cecilia*] *Metella Wife* [*of Crassus*]
Gouache
Bianchi was a more celebrated artist than Busiri, but better known as a figure-painter, like his teacher Benedetto Luti (1666–1724) – from whom, however, he also learnt to do landscape capriccios in gouache. Perhaps Windham originally wanted Bianchi rather than Busiri to paint a set for him, but found him unable to.

37 CORNELIS SAFTLEVEN (1607–81)
Two cows in a byre
Ascribed to this Rotterdam painter of landscapes and genre scenes in the style of David Teniers the Younger in the hanging-plan and 1764 and 1771 inventories. He is also believed to have worked for Rubens in Antwerp.

WINDOW BAY, RIGHT WALL (BOTTOM TO TOP):

38 LUCAS VAN VALCKENBORCH (*c.*1535–97)
A View on the Meuse with miners
Inscribed: *P. BRILL*
Ascribed to the better-known Paul Bril (1554–1626), because of the false inscription, until identified as by this precursor of him. Both Lucas and his brother Maerten (1542–1612) painted a number of sites on the Meuse around Liège, not far from their native Louvain, which are not only amongst the earliest purely topographical paintings in Europe, but also show the exploitation of some of Europe's first coal-mines.

*A View on the
Meuse with miners;
by Lucas van
Valckenborch
(Cabinet)*

39 PIETRO BIANCHI (1694–1740)
[*Washerwomen at a fountain amongst Antique ruins*]
Gouache
Pendant to no.36.

40 ? VENETIAN, mid-eighteenth-century
The Agony in the Garden
Called 'supposed C. Maratt' in Windham's hanging-plan, and simply ascribed to Maratta thereafter, but it cannot be by this artist, nor even Roman. It is more probably from the northern Veneto or the Tyrol.

RETURN WALL, RIGHT OF WINDOW BAY:

41, 42 G. B. BUSIRI, pair of gouaches (bottom to top):
[*View on the road to Terni*]; *View of the Cascatelle at Tivoli and the Temple of the Sybil*

LEFT OF CHIMNEY-PIECE, FAR LEFT:

43–5 G. B. BUSIRI, three gouaches (bottom to top):
View in Italy [*River with double weir and weird rocks*]; *Temple of Vesta in the mouth of the Cloaca Maxima at Rome*; *Tomb of Cecilia Metella, wife of Crassus, near Rome, called Capo di Bove*

CENTRE COLUMN (BOTTOM TO TOP):

46 Attributed to EGBERT VAN DER POEL (1621–64)
Fishermen selling their catch on the beach
Not originally here or in the Drawing Room, hence the black slip needed to fit it into the frame, which does belong in these rooms. There was originally another *Squall* by Van de Velde here, balancing the one that has had to be taken off the door.

47 JAN BAPTIST HUYSMANS (1654–1716)
Valley landscape with a grieving woman and companions
Pendant to no.5.

48 KAREL VAN VOGELAER, called CARLO DEI FIORI (1653–95)
Vase of Flowers

NEAR LEFT OF CHIMNEY-PIECE:

49–51 G. B. BUSIRI, three gouaches (bottom to top):
Antique Tomb vulgarly called Nero's; *Ruin of the Temple of Minerva Medica at Rome*; *Sepulchre of the 3 Horatii and 3 Curatii at Albano*

FURNITURE

Nearly all the original 1750s furniture of the Cabinet was disposed of in 1918 but appears in early photographs. The 1771 inventory records '2 Large Mahogany Settees, carved and covered with Crimson Damask. 2 Bolsters to Each. 10 Large Mahogany arm Chairs Covered with Crimson Damask. 3 Stools of the same and Covers to all of Crimson Baize'. The legs and arms were carved with Chinoiserie lattice and the seat rails were scalloped. The present furniture is as follows:

The gilded overmantel mirror and picture frame, ordered from John Bladwell in March 1752.

The splendid Rococo pier-table was made by a leading London craftsman, perhaps James Whittle or Thomas Chippendale. The Siena marble top was supplied by Thomas Carter. On 30 April 1752 Windham wrote, 'I have seen the new Chimney for the Cabinet. I have bespoke also a table for that room all which will be ready in about a month tho I shall hasten them all I can . . .'

Pair of ormolu candle branches (the other pair is in the Drawing Room).

The two gilded plaster brackets on either side of the window bay, representing Apollo and, possibly, Daphne, have been attributed to John Cheere and are also original (the other larger pair is in the Drawing Room).

French Boulle commode with three drawers, early eighteenth-century.

The five French-style upholstered mahogany chairs with carved cabriole legs are of c.1750 but were brought down from what is now the Red Bedroom in c.1830 by Admiral Windham for his Drawing Room (hence the Drawing Room damask on two of them).

A black lacquer eighteenth-century oriental cabinet on a modern stand.

Two French Boulle cabinets with black marble tops, early nineteenth-century.

Circular rosewood centre-table with brass inlay, c.1830.

Four giltwood torchères, one of which bears the label of William Freeman of Norwich, c.1830 (the Neo-classical candlesticks are contemporary).

Two early nineteenth-century giltwood stands incorporating Sèvres porcelain dishes.

A giltwood table with an inlaid marble chessboard top, nineteenth-century.

Four French-style armchairs in white and gilt with needlepoint covers incorporating the initials 'H', 'CH' and 'CW'.

An oriental lacquer cabinet on an English mahogany stand of c.1750.

French Boulle *Bureau Mazarin*, late seventeenth-century.

CERAMICS

Bow harlequin of c.1752 based on Meissen original.

Bow Benedictine monk, c.1755.

Two Plymouth shells, c.1770, based on a Bow original.

Two Dehua *blanc-de-Chine* libation cups, late seventeenth- or early eighteenth-century, based on rhinoceros horn originals.

The remaining china is mainly nineteenth-century Chinese *famille rose* and small English cache-pots, c.1800–10.

CLOCK

Fourteen-day striking mantel clock in ormolu and marble case, signed 'De Belle, Rue St Honoré, A Paris', c.1790. The white marble base, incorporating an aneroid barometer and two thermometers, was added c.1870.

CHANDELIER

Crystal gasolier, later nineteenth-century.

CARPET

William Windham II's 'Wilton carpet which covers the room' was replaced c.1851 by the present 'English Savonnerie' carpet.

THE STONE CORRIDOR

This and the West Corridor above are an extension built by William Windham II in 1751–2. The watercloset at the Cabinet end was added by Robert Brettingham in 1788. The eighteenth-century decoration is not known, but in the later nineteenth century this, like other service corridors and attic stairs, was painted a rich red. The present scheme is modern.

PICTURES

LEFT-HAND WALL:

Manner of MARMADUKE CRADOCK
(c.1660–1716/17)
Poultry and pheasants in a formal garden

NORWICH SCHOOL, late eighteenth-century
Norwich Castle

RIGHT-HAND WALL:

ENGLISH, eighteenth-century
Portrait of a lion

Manner of MARMADUKE CRADOCK
(c.1660–1716/17)
Hen and chicks before a cottage

CHARLES G. LEWIS after THOMAS JONES
BARKER (1815–82)
The Duke of Cambridge and Lord Raglan, with French officers, directing the Siege of Sebastopol, 1855

SCULPTURE

– DENIÈRE after an Unknown Sculptor in the manner of CLODION
Five Bacchic Putti playing with a goat
Bronze. Signed: DENIÈRE and *Clodion*
The first signature is that of the bronze-founder, but the second signature is not authentic. This is a nineteenth-century pastiche of a favourite eighteenth-century subject.

CHRISTOPHE FRATIN (1800–64)
Two stags in combat
Bronze. Signed: FRATIN
The original of this group was rejected from the Paris Salon of 1840.

CHRISTOPHE FRATIN (1800–64)
Standing bull and recumbent cow
Bronze. Signed: FRATIN

FURNITURE

Four mahogany dining-tables, mid-eighteenth-century.

The walnut chairs with simple pierced splats in two patterns may be some of the 'Walnut Tree Chairs With Leather Bottoms' listed in the Dining Room in 1771 (see p.51, and also Great Hall and West Corridor).

A series of fine mahogany chairs with scroll-pattern backs related to the pattern books of Robert Mainwaring (others are in the West Corridor above).

One of them has stamped on the original webbing the initials 'T.G.'. They are probably the 'Mahogany chairs with Crimson Damask Bottoms' listed in 1771 in the Great Parlour (now Drawing Room).

A good oriental lacquer cabinet on a painted English stand of c.1720, whose shell decorations are characteristically neo-Palladian.

China cabinet in Sheraton style, late nineteenth-century.

Mahogany chest-on-chest of c.1750.

CERAMICS AND GLASS

IN SHERATON-STYLE CABINET:

Collection of glasses mainly dating from the mid-eighteenth century, as well as late eighteenth-century Chinese export porcelain. Of particular interest are two bourdalous (slipper chamberpots), one Chinese, c.1720, the other with flowers, Boisette, c.1780.

THE STAIR HALL

The construction of James Paine's Stair Hall was begun in the spring of 1752. It occupied much of the site of the 1680s stairs but actually achieved fewer and more gradual flights in a smaller space. Paine's design, for which the drawing survives, was closely related to his Dining Room and Great Hall in its use of plaster decoration and bronzed plaster casts. It included a timber and plaster barrel vault, lit at either end by semi-circular 'therm' windows. This exerted too much thrust on the side walls and was replaced in 1813 by Humphry Repton and his son John Adey with a more conventional skylight (subsequently removed). One further change from Paine's drawings was made during the course of construction in June 1752, when Windham cancelled the medals which had been made to go over the north doors on the gallery in favour of two more busts. That is why the *rocaille* brackets are different from the rest. In the same month ale was given to the stonecutters to celebrate the completion of the floor here and in the Stone Corridor. The plasterwork seems to have been finished by November but it was not until June 1753 that Thomas Wagg, described by Windham as 'a top master-workman' who 'lives in a very good way', was able to install his beautiful iron balustrading.

DECORATION

The Stair Hall was redecorated for Admiral Windham in 1824 by Dixon of Norwich. There is a general resemblance to Paine's Dining Room scheme but with less attractive colours.

PICTURES

(Beginning with left-hand overdoor, and thereafter clockwise, ascending the stair, top picture described before that below it.)

Most of the portraits here came from Beeston Regis, the Norfolk seat from the eighteenth to the twentieth centuries of the Cremer family. However, they are not a coherent group, and none is inscribed. Indeed it is perfectly possible that they came with, and depict, members of the Green and Woodrow families, and of others with which the Cremers had also intermarried.

After JAN LIEVENS (1607–74)
Miser casting his accounts
Once thought to be by Rembrandt, this is instead a copy of a picture now in the Heinz Kisters collection in Kreuzlingen, by a contemporary of Rembrandt, whom he both influenced and was influenced by.

Manner of FRANS SNYDERS (1579–1657)
Hounds harassing a wild boar

GEORGE CLINT, ARA (1770–1854)
Rear-Admiral William Windham (previously Lukin)
Exhibited at the RA in 1825, the year after Felbrigg had finally passed to him on the death of William Windham's widow, and he had taken the name of Windham in gratitude.

Studio of Sir GODFREY KNELLER, Bt (1646/9–1723)
Hester Buckworth (d.1708)
The fiancée and love of Ashe Windham's life, before her sudden death from smallpox. The image is taken from a signed portrait of her father, *Sir John Buckworth and his family*, that was latterly in the collection of Sir Arthur Bryant.

ENGLISH, mid-eighteenth-century
? Edmund Cremer (d.1786)
Son of William Cremer, he inherited Ingoldisthorpe from his remote cousin Francis, and married another cousin, Mary Green, around 1745. They left no surviving children, and the Cremer name endured thanks only to the grandson of her sister

Lucy, who abandoned the name of Woodrow for that of Cremer.

ENGLISH, later eighteenth-century
? Mary Ellis, Mrs Cremer Woodrow
Called Mary Cremer, wife and cousin of the above, but she is clearly of a whole generation later than him. Possibly, therefore, the daughter of Richard Ellis of Runton, and the wife of Cremer Woodrow (b.1746), Mary Cremer's nephew.

ENGLISH, early eighteenth-century
? Francis Cremer (d.c.1759) and *? Mary Green, Mrs Cremer* (d. before 1744/5)
Pair of ovals
In 1714 Francis Cremer married Mary Green, daughter and heir of Robert Green, who brought Beeston into the family. They had two daughters: Mary, the wife of Edmund Cremer (see above); and Lucy, who married Thomas Woodrow, whose grandson assumed the name of Cremer.

NORWICH SCHOOL, c.1800
An estuary by moonlight

Attributed to ISAAC FULLER (active 1644–72)
Called *Edmund Cremer of Snettisham* (d.c.1672)
Second son of Thomas Cremer of Snettisham and Joan Hargate; married Alice Bragge in 1623, and resided at Lynn Regis (King's Lynn). Said to have been 'a man of Puritan convictions, who was active as a Justice of the Peace during the Commonwealth years.' But the skull-cap denotes a clergyman, and the portrait was painted c.1650–60, when Edmund Cremer would have been older than this sitter, so the identification is unreliable.

ENGLISH, later seventeenth-century
A Gentleman in armour, said to be Francis Cremer (b.1653/4)
If rightly named, then this would be Francis Cremer of Ingoldisthorpe, elder son of another Francis (1626/7–86) and Margaret Pell of Dersingham.

Manner of Sir ANTHONY VAN DYCK (1599–1641)
Unknown Royalist in a cuirass (? Sir John Cremer d.c.1667/8)
One of the finest portraits from Beeston. It dates from the 1650s, and the blue-and-gold sash suggests that the sitter had taken service with the Dutch, after the failure of the Royalist cause. It may be, however, that a confusion occurred, and that this is Sir John Cremer of Seche(y) or Setch, and not the portrait higher up the stairs once impossibly vested with his name (see below). He was the eldest son

of George Cremer of Seche and Elizabeth, daughter of Adam Williamson of Keswick, and married, firstly, Sarah, daughter of the Royalist Sir Edward Filmer, in 1638; and secondly, Ursula Fabian, in 1661/2. In 1660 he was Sheriff of Norfolk and knighted.

ENGLISH, mid-seventeenth-century
? Rev. Thomas Cremer
Reputedly Thomas Cremer, Rector of Grimston, *c.*1660.

ENGLISH, *c.*1675/85
? Francis Cremer of Ingoldisthorpe
Painted too late to be of Sir John Cremer (above). Ketton-Cremer therefore suggested that it might instead be of Francis Cremer of Ingoldisthorpe (1626/7–86), husband of Margaret Pell (d.1680) of

Dersingham, and of two succeeding wives, and father of another Francis Cremer (above).

MARY (CRADOCK) BEALE (1633–99)
? The Rev. William Cremer (1663/4–1736)
Signed: *Maria Beale Pinxit*
When at Beeston, this was known as the Rev. Robert Cremer (d.1767), Vicar of Wymondham. His dates make this impossible, but the sitter may be, as Ketton-Cremer suggested, the Rev. William Cremer (1663/4–1736), the second son of another William Cremer, and of Elizabeth Finch of Cambridge, painted around 1692.

JOHN SHACKLETON (active 1742–d.1767)
'Count' James Dagnia (*c.*1708/9–55)
Long misidentified as Benjamin Stillingfleet (1702–71), the impoverished scholar, botanist, and

The Stair Hall

tutor, then friend, of William Windham II. The character of the frame proclaims it to be the portrait of '*Mr Dagnia*' by Shackleton recorded over the chimney-piece in the Drawing Room in the inventories of 1764 and 1771. Dagnia is a mysterious figure whose relationship with Windham is obscure: it is otherwise known only from a drawing for the bow of the Cabinet (see p.23), and from a report of his death from Shackleton and Stillingfleet. He was from a family of glass manufacturers of Italian origin who had settled at Cleadon, Co. Durham, where his father had bought an estate and built Cleadon Hall. Known as 'the famous gentleman glassblower' and 'the gentleman painter' (see the picture opposite), he figured as 'Count Dagnia' in Rome, where he was much patronised by English noblemen, and where it is probable that his friendship with Windham was formed.

? JAMES DAGNIA (*c.*1708/9–55)
William Windham II (1717–61) as a young man in the costume of a Hussar
A head-and-shoulders engraving (1810) gives the painter as Shackleton, but this may be a confusion with the picture opposite (see above). The composition is based on Worlidge's *David Garrick as Tancred* (V&A). This portrait seems to have given rise to the legend that, when on his travels (1738–42), Windham served as an officer in the Empress Maria Theresa's regiment of Hungarian Hussars. This is inherently improbable, but the complete nature of his costume here suggests more than fancy dress, and that he actually possessed the real thing. It may be another indication that he did get as far as Vienna and Hungary. After Maria Theresa's coronation as Queen of Hungary in 1741, the Hungarians became her stoutest defenders, and the Hussars popular symbols of this for her English allies. What may have been this portrait was recorded in Dagnia's hands at his death.

SCULPTURE

After the Antique, nineteenth-century
Boy pulling a thorn out of his foot ('Il Spinario')
Marble
A late copy of a celebrated Antique bronze that was already known in the twelfth century, and has been in the Palazzo dei Conservatori on the Capitol in Rome since the fifteenth century.

The busts in bronzed plaster on brackets in the blank oculi are real or imagined likenesses of Ancient Greeks and Romans by John Cheere (like those in the Dining Room), and represent (clockwise, starting over the Library door): *Seneca*, ? *Sappho*, ? *Horace*, ? *Faustina*, ? *Virgil*, *Cicero*, *Antinous*.

FURNITURE

BENEATH STAIRS:

An armchair and two side-chairs of *c.*1690. Among the earliest pieces in the house and probably acquired by Katherine Windham.

A large mahogany bookcase with glazed doors and a richly moulded cornice, *c.*1740.

Gong and stand, *c.*1850.

ON HALF-LANDING:

Five Chinese Chippendale pattern chairs with cane seats, *c.*1750.

ON GALLERY:

Four Chinese Chippendale chairs of a slightly different pattern (belonging to the set in the Chinese Bedroom) *c.*1750, and a seventeenth-century oak chest.

CLOCKS

AT FOOT OF STAIRS:

Eight-day longcase clock by John Snow of London in a Chinese lacquer case, *c.*1730.

ON GALLERY:

Eight-day striking clock by Joseph Herring of London in a Chinese lacquer case, *c.*1750.

LANTERN

Possibly the one listed in the Great Hall in 1771.

CARPET

The stair carpet is a 1992 reweaving of the late Victorian stair runner. Care was taken to reproduce the colours in their original intensity.

THE LIBRARY

This was probably the Great Chamber of the Jacobean house and was made into the Library by William Windham II in 1752–5. Windham's object was to house the books which he had bought on the Grand Tour as well as those of his father and

The Library

grandfather. His remark in a letter of 18 June 1752, 'I think the library should be nearly as that at Blickling is . . .' was evidently reconsidered. Blickling's Long Gallery, fitted out to take the books in 1745, made extensive use of John Cheere's busts, which clearly influenced Windham in the decoration of his Dining Room, Great Hall and Stair Hall. But in the Library he appears ultimately to have abandoned the Blickling model, whose design was classical, in favour of a Gothick interior, considered appropriate to the character of the old south front.

Paine's oak bookcases were being finished by George Church in January 1755, when a dispute over incorrect measurements and the difficulty of fitting the pinnacles produced an indignant letter from the craftsman. The old west bay window was blocked and shelved up in 1787 by William Windham III, who needed more space for his books. At this time it appears that the panels of tracery decoration, based on the design of the 1750s library table (see below), were added to the presses. The architect of these changes was Robert Furze Brettingham.

Wyndham Ketton-Cremer recalls his visits to this room as a boy in the 1920s:

The shelves bore the scars of the sale [see p.34] . . . and the gaps in the rows of calf and vellum were filled with the strangest miscellany of substitutes – cheap novels, old Bradshaws and Baedeckers, copies of *Kelly's Directory* and *Whitaker's Almanac*, volumes of the *Badminton Library* and *Punch*. The sun would pour in through the unshaded windows, cracking and fading the bindings that it reached. Flies buzzed against the panes, the only sound in the silence of the room. . . .'

FIREPLACE

The veined marble bolection-moulded surround of *c.*1685 came originally from the Caroline Great Parlour and was moved here because, as Windham wrote in January 1752, 'It is of bilection work more in the old taste.' Paine had planned a new fireplace flanked by neo-Jacobean terms. The grate and dogs are mid-nineteenth-century, as is the oak overmantel.

The Library still contains many of William Windham II's books, which reflect his interest in architecture, natural history, military drill, wood-turning and fireworks

CEILING

Part of the 1750s ceiling remains in the south bay, but most of it, badly damaged by a leaky roof, was removed in 1923. Paine's drawing for a neo-Jacobean fret of squares and octagons, which he sent to the plasterer George Green in August 1752, fortunately survives. The ceiling of the shelved-up west bay is a paraphrase of Paine's design (which remains above it) by Cato and Swaine of Norwich, carried out in 1788/9.

BOOKS

A number of volumes survive from the time of William Windham I and his son Ashe. William's are identifiable by his fine armorial bookplate. In one of her notebooks, his wife Katherine listed her books, which included a stout volume of plays by Dryden, Otway, Wycherley and other contemporary dramatists, which still remains in the library. Other works from this early period include manuals of piety such as *The Whole Duty of Man*, or more practical volumes on physic, cookery and gardening, including Evelyn's *Sylva*.

William Windham II formed the core of the collection now at Felbrigg. His interests in architecture, the sciences and languages are reflected in his purchases. Many of the large folios on architecture and classical antiquities were bought on his prolonged Grand Tour of 1738–42. While in Geneva he acquired a copy of Gauffecourt's *Traité de la reliure*, and he also owned a large outfit of binders' tools and materials (see p.80). Around 300 volumes of miscellaneous pamphlets containing poems, plays, scientific and mathematical treatises were probably bound on the premises under his supervision. Quite a few still include instructions to a binder in his hand. Besides being an avid reader, Windham was himself the author of a number of pamphlets, ranging from a lively squib against Smollett's translation of *Don Quixote* to an immensely elaborate training manual, *A Plan of Discipline* (1759), for the county militia. Another rarity is the manuscript of *Ragandjaw*, a short satirical play written by David Garrick and dedicated to Windham in 1746.

William Windham III added greatly to his father's collection of books, particularly in the fields of literature, philosophy, politics and economics. Still to be found here are Dr Johnson's own copies of the *Iliad*, *Odyssey* and *New Testament*, which he inherited from his friend, with eighteen other volumes bought at the sale of Johnson's effects in 1785. Apart from Windham's own early diaries, edited by R. W. Ketton-Cremer, two volumes of particular interest are Nathaniel Kent's agricultural treatises of 1775 and 1796, based to a large extent on his management and planting of the Felbrigg estate on Windham's behalf.

Comparatively few books were added to the collection by Admiral Lukin or his son William Howe Windham, described as a 'rough unlettered squire'. The bulk of modern collecting activity can be found in the working library of R. W. Ketton-Cremer (see p.35).

(see p.35).

FURNITURE

In 1771 the main items of furniture in the Library were:

a Very Large Handsome Mahogany Library Table, 2 Large Wainscot Tables, with Wire Doors, 1 Mahogany Claw Table, a Mahogany table of a Less Size, a Mahogany press, 2 Mahogany Settees Covered With Black Callimanco, 6 Mahogany Armchairs Covered With the Same, 2 Chairs with Leather Bottoms . . .

The furniture today:

Truncated mahogany whatnot, claw table and reading stand, *c.*1750.

IN WEST BAY:

Mahogany library table with drawers and tracery decoration, one of two made to Paine's design by George Church in 1753 for £21 (see p.24).

(see p.24).

ON DESK:

Seventeenth-century oak writing slope.

Celestial and terrestrial globes on satinwood veneer stands made by J. & W. Cary of 181, The Strand in 1799 and 1814 respectively.

Heavy, carved octagonal oak centre table, *c.*1850.

AT TABLES IN CENTRE AND IN WINDOW BAY:

Set of walnut chairs, *c.*1730, with modern flame-stitch canvas embroidered seats.

Two mahogany upholstered armchairs covered in black leathercloth, *c.*1750.

Oval drop-leaf table, *c.*1730.

BRONZE

Napoleon, nineteenth-century

CARPET

Fitted carpet with floral bouquets against a green background, *c.*1830.

THE BOOK ROOM

Entered through a concealed jib-door in one of the presses, this was Sarah Windham's bedroom in the 1750s, and, as the 1771 inventory records, had an embroidered bed lined with green silk, a suite of seat furniture covered in green damask with green and white checked case covers and 'a Large Mahogany Case for China or Books' (now in the Stair Hall), as well as a 'Ewe Tree Bureau with Looking Glass Doors' (now in the Morning Room). The walls were hung with green flowered paper and the adjacent 'light closet' furnished with two damask-covered stools and a mahogany table.

All this was changed in the 1780s when the statesman William Windham III turned this into a convenient sitting-room. The diarist Joseph Farington records, 'The Library is upstairs, and in a room adjoining it Mr Windham always sat when engaged in business or study. . . . During this time he slept in a small tent bed put up in a niche in a room next to His sitting room, for the convenience of it being near the Library.' The Gothick plaster frieze, probably designed by Robert Brettingham, dates from this period.

In the 1930s the room became R. W. Ketton-Cremer's study and after the transfer of the property to the National Trust, part of a staff flat. In 1986 it was furnished as a place for the display of archival material and books from the Library. The bookcases hold what remains at Felbrigg of the last squire's working library, most of which now forms the Ketton-Cremer Collection at the University of East Anglia.

PICTURES

OVERMANTEL:

After JOHANN ZOFFANY (1733–1810)
Robert Marsham, FRS (1708–97)
Squire of Stratton Strawless, friend of William Windham II and Benjamin Stillingfleet, and correspondent in his old age of Gilbert White of Selborne,

Marsham was a passionate planter and cultivator of trees. The original of *c*.1761 is at Hardingham Hall.

Around the walls is a variety of drawings and water-colours of Norfolk and – in particular – Felbrigg, ranging from the eighteenth to the twentieth century, and mostly signed or labelled. Between the Bay Room and the Library door is a Roman seventeenth-century pen drawing (by a follower of Carlo Maratta) of a *Vision of St Carlo Borromeo*; and below, a pen and wash design for a ceiling (intended for Felbrigg?), by Sir James Thornhill.

SCULPTURE

ON CHIMNEY-PIECE:

Two nineteenth-century bronzes after the Antique, of the *Apollo Belvedere* and the *Diana of Fontainebleau*.

FURNITURE

The display cabinets and bookcases were designed by John Bedford and made by Daniel Windham.

THE GREY DRESSING ROOM

The door to the Grey Dressing Room brings us back into the 1680s wing. Its angled entrance results from the projection of one of the Jacobean Hall chimneystacks. In order to create a rectangular plan, Paine reduced the size of the room, allowing generous storage space in the embrasure, which on the upper level produced a concealed cupboard which contains a fragment of the 1680s Stair Hall ceiling. The cupboard and the entrance are closed by an unusually tall single jib-door.

This modest room, panelled out by George Church in 1753, was used by William Windham II as his dressing-room (see p.25). It was simply furnished in 1771 with 'a Mahogany Chest of Draws, a Wainscot Clothes Press with Draws, an Armchair covered in Black Callimanco, a Chair covered with leather, a Looking Glass with a Small Mahogany Frame, a Green Harriteen Window Curtain.'

FIREPLACE

A simple surround in veined marble, tiled, like that in China Room, with a narrow mouth for a stove. Windham wrote in May 1753, 'I think a brass stove in my dressing room is the very thing I should like

let it not be a very small one for the sake of airing things.'

FURNITURE

A fine Rococo mirror of *c*.1750, now painted grey and probably supplied by John Bladwell.

Slipper bath, nineteenth-century. This impractical object had already been banished to a lumber room by 1863.

Mahogany pot cupboard, *c*.1800.

Iron and brass bed, *c*.1900.

A mahogany tallboy of *c*.1750 with Rococo escutcheons.

Papier-mâché table, *c*.1850.

CERAMICS

Ewer and footbath by Minton, *c*.1900.

CARPET

Ferraghan, modern.

THE YELLOW BEDROOM

This was 'The Green Bedchamber' in 1771 with a crimson and green silk damask bed, walnut chairs with matching seats, curtains of green lutestring (a glossy silk) and a flowered green wallpaper. Like the Grey Dressing Room, it was formed out of the old Stair Hall and all the architectural detail is of 1752–3.

DECORATION

The room was repainted in the 1970s to recreate a pre-existing 1920s scheme of R. W. Ketton-Cremer's parents.

FIREPLACE

Contemporary with the room but with a register grate of *c*.1790.

PICTURES

The papier-mâché frames on the Kessel and Alpine scene may be the work of René Duffour, who supplied carved and gilded work to Windham in the early 1750s and whose trade card described him as a specialist in this medium.

FROM RIGHT OF DOOR TO ROSE BEDROOM:

BARTHÉLÉMY DU PAN (1712–63)
William Windham II (1717–61) as a young man
Pastel
Painted either in Geneva, where Windham was from 1738 to 1742, with interruptions, or in England, to which du Pan came (perhaps encouraged by the young 'Bloods' of the 'Common Room') from 1743 to 1750; but the youth of the sitter, and his brilliant dress, suggest the former.

Attributed to JOSEPH STANNARD (1797–1830)
Norfolk beach scene
Acquired by Ketton-Cremer at the sale of The Grove, Diss, 10 January 1935.

JAN VAN KESSEL (1641/2–80)
A bleaching-ground outside Haarlem
Signed: *J: van Kessel*
Kessel was a friend of Hobbema, and possibly a pupil of Jacob van Ruisdael, a number of whose views of his native Haarlem show the grounds where laundry was left to be dried and bleached by the sun. Probably acquired by William Windham II in the Low Countries on his return from Switzerland in the autumn of 1742.

? SWISS, ? eighteenth-century
Imaginary scene in the Alps

? SAMUEL DAVID COLKETT (1806–63)
A track beside a cottage in a wood
Painted in 1852 by 'Colkirk', according to an old label and inscription on the back of the panel, but no painter is recorded with that name, which is probably a misreading or mistranscription of Colkett's.

Attributed to PETER MONAMY (1680/1–1748/9)
Four British warships and a fishing-smack in a strong wind
Monamy modelled himself on the younger Van de Velde, and his works are not always easy to tell from other imitations of the latter.

ABRAHAM STORCK (1644–1708/10)
A whaler and other ships at anchor before a port
Signed
This is similar in format to the two pictures in the Cabinet, and was evidently also acquired by Admiral Lukin, but is a more purely marine painting.

DUTCH, *c.*1800.
Ships in a calm off a quay
Panel
A later imitation of a Van de Velde.

ENGLISH, nineteenth-century
George Wyndham (1762–1810)
Oval
Father of Marianne Wyndham, who married the Rev. Cremer Cremer. Although put in an eighteenth-century frame, this appears to be a later pastiche, done from a miniature in the collection, of *c.*1770/80.

? The Rev. JAMES WILLS (active 1740–d.1777)
Sarah Hicks, Mrs William Windham, formerly Mrs Lukin (1710–92)
Pastel. Signed: *J W 1754*
Sarah Hicks of Tanfield, Essex had been left a widow with three children by her first husband, Robert Lukin, of Dunmow in the same county, in 1744. Because of his father's disapproval, she was at first only William Windham II's mistress, but, after the death of the former in 1749 and her expectation of a child – the future William Windham III – they were married in 1750.

FURNITURE

Mahogany dressing-table and matching washstand, *c.*1830.

BETWEEN WINDOWS:

Fine gilded pier-glass of *c.*1750 by John Bladwell (the glass is late seventeenth-century).

Armchair *c.*1850, with 1920s chintz cover.

Sofa of *c.*1750 with 1920s chintz cover.

Upholstered side-chair of *c.*1750.

Gothic mahogany wardrobe, *c.*1860.

Mahogany full tester bed, *c.*1830, with modern chintz hangings.

Mahogany pot cupboard, *c.*1750.

CERAMICS

Washstand set, Spode, late nineteenth-century.

THE ROSE BEDROOM

This room appears to have been first fitted out in 1705 (see p.18). The bolection-moulded dado panelling is of that time, if somewhat reorganised, and so is the timber cornice. The doors are of an early eighteenth-century pattern. Two are modern copies of doors which found their way into Donthorn's stables. The two beside the fireplace are original. It was described as the 'Middle Dressing Room' in 1771, when it had a flowered red paper (like the contemporary decoration of the Great Parlour beneath) and rich furniture covered in crimson damask.

CEILING

The plaster cove and border seem to contain elements by Edward Goudge of c.1687, but it is probable that they were all salvaged from the Great Stairs ceiling and rearranged here by c.1752–3 by George Green, who showed such facility in

The Rose Bedroom

manipulating the Caroline plasterwork in the Cabinet. There are noticeable differences in design and workmanship, especially between the garlands over the fireplace wall, suspended from rings and hooks, as opposed to the knots of drapery used in the other coves. The border of laurel and oak is also reused 1680s work.

FIREPLACE

Veined marble surround of 1752–3 with iron grate of c.1850.

PICTURES

ON WALL TO YELLOW BEDROOM, NEAR TO FAR:

Manner of WILLIAM VAN DE VELDE the Younger (1633–1707)
Three ships in a squall
Bears initials *W V V*
Removed, for safety, from the door of the Cabinet Room, in one of that room's characteristic Rococo frames.

Manner of FRANCESCO ZUCCARELLI (1702–88)
Pastoral figures amongst ruins beside a river
The pendant of a similar picture in the Drawing Room.

ROBERT LADBROOKE (1769–1842)
Beeston Regis from the 'Roman Camp'
Panel, with transferred inscription on the back:
Ladbroke pinxit
Beeston, as Ketton-Cremer noted on the back, is portrayed with a considerable degree of artistic licence. The later Cremer seat was at Beeston.

HUMPHRY REPTON (1752–1818)
William Windham III making his maiden speech at Norwich, 1778
Windham entered politics by drawing up a petition to oppose the war against the American colonies. Repton began his career as Windham's political assistant.

FURNITURE

Mahogany half-tester bed with contemporary hangings, washstand, dressing-table, wardrobe and curtain pelmets, c.1840.

Two white and gilt pier-glasses of c.1752 by John Bladwell, made to accommodate late seventeenth-century mirror glass whose bevels are discernible.

Two mahogany pot cupboards of c.1820.

Large sofa of *c*.1750 with serpentine back and traces of red damask beneath the present modern loose cover. No doubt the one mentioned in the 1771 inventory of this room.

Cheval glass, *c*.1820.

Two upholstered side-chairs (covers Victorian), contemporary with the sofa and part of the suite.

Fine mahogany writing-table, *c*.1830.

Two easy chairs of *c*.1820 with Victorian loose covers.

Victorian prie-dieu with needlework cover.

CLOCKS

Nineteenth-century eight-day French striking mantel clock, showing the day, date and month on separate dials, and temperature in Fahrenheit and Centigrade, by Devin, Paris.

CARPETS

Ferraghan rugs, modern.

THE RED BEDROOM

Here the dado panelling and cornice are of *c*.1705 and the former noticeably more elaborate than in the Rose Bedroom. In 1771 this had become a well-appointed bedchamber with flowered grey paper, a 'Very Rich White Silk Damask Bed' with 'Mahogany Bed Posts Carved' (sold in 1918) and six mahogany armchairs (probably the smaller ones now in the Cabinet) covered with the same material as the bed.

DECORATION

The room was last decorated *c*.1860. The rich flock and gilt wallpaper is of this period but has lost much of its colour. The buff stripes were once candy pink. The gilt cord survives from the 1750s decoration.

FIREPLACE

Grey-veined marble chimney-piece of *c*.1750 with contemporary carved wood surround and mantel shelf. Grate *c*.1830.

PICTURES

LEFT OF ENTRANCE DOOR:

HUGH DOUGLAS HAMILTON (1736–1808)
? *William Windham III* (1750–1810)
Pastel. Oval. Signed and dated *1773* on the back
Acquired at a sale in Wymondham in 1974.

FROM OVER DOOR TO CHINESE BEDROOM, CLOCKWISE:

? LOUIS LAGUERRE (1663–1721)
Cain supervising the building of the walls of Enoch
This unusual subject was set for the French Academy of Painting and Sculpture's competition in 1682. It appears to be by the joint third-prize winner, who came over to England two years later; indeed he may have brought it with him to show his ability, before going on to become the foremost decorative painter over here.

ENGLISH, late sixteenth-century
Francis Windham (d.1592)
Panel. Inscribed with details of his career
Chief Justice of the Common Pleas, from 1579. Second son of Sir Edmund Windham of Felbrigg by Susan Townshend. Bought by Ketton-Cremer at the sale of Heydon Hall in July 1949.

? ENGLISH, ? eighteenth-century
Portrait of a Turk
Apparently an exercise in the manner of Rembrandt's studies of Orientals.

ENGLISH, *c*.1800
Portrait of an Unknown Man
A good picture, in the manner of Hoppner, probably of a member of the Cremer or Wyndham families.

ENGLISH, *c*.1800
Venus lamenting the dead Adonis
A daub.

ENGLISH, *c*.1800
Portrait of a Lady
Probably the wife of the man facing her. She is holding a shuttle and a thread, and seems to be in mourning.

CHARLES CATTON the Elder (1728–98)
John Buckle (d.1818)
Sheriff of Norfolk in 1787 and Mayor of Norwich in 1793. He was uncle of Anne Buckle, Mrs Cremer, whose portrait is below. He is shown writing in his daybooks.

ENGLISH, *c.*1800/5
Anne Buckle, Mrs Cremer Cremer (1772–1860)
Oval
Daughter of Thrower Buckle and co-heiress of John Buckle of Cringleford, and Ketton-Cremer's great-great-grandmother.

JOHN THEODORE HEINS Senior (1697–1756)
The meeting of Abraham and Melchizedek
Signed: *Heins Pinx^t.*, and inscribed: *David & Ahimelech / I Samuel*
A much simplified copy of a reversed engraving of Rubens's picture now in the museum at Caen. Despite the misleading inscription, this shows the priest-king of Salem blessing the victorious Abraham and bringing him bread and wine, which was later regarded as a prefiguration of the Eucharist (*Genesis*, xiv, 18–20).

ENGLISH, *c.*1800/05
Cremer Cremer (1768–1808)
Oval
Born Cremer Woodrow, and took the surname Cremer by royal licence. Ketton-Cremer's great-great-grandfather.

? SPANISH, seventeenth-century
The Madonna and Child, with SS Elizabeth and John the Baptist and a child-angel
Probably the 'Picture of the Holy Family' listed in the Red Dressing Room in 1771.

FURNITURE

BETWEEN WINDOWS:

Fine Rococo gilt pier-glass of *c.*1752, by John Bladwell, with seventeenth-century glass.

Mahogany work table with lyre legs of *c.*1810.

Bed steps incorporating pot cupboard, *c.*1830.

Mahogany full-tester bed of *c.*1830 with contemporary chintz hangings.

Rosewood writing-table, *c.*1830.

Mahogany pot cupboard, *c.*1820.

Fine Neo-classical mahogany commode with marble top and gilt mounts, *c.*1830.

Sabre-legged tub chair of the same date.

Overmantel glass, *c.*1752. In September 1751 Windham wrote, 'I find it is a high fashion for oval glasses to be placed over chimneys, and carved work around them,' and this mirror resembles one of Paine's designs for a fireplace at Felbrigg.

Ormolu and bronze candelabra, *c.*1850.

Mid-eighteenth-century mahogany pole-screen with contemporary needlework.

Cheval glass, mahogany, *c.*1820.

Gentleman's wardrobe in mahogany veneer and other woods, *c.*1790.

Two upholstered mahogany side-chairs, *c.*1750 (part of the original suite for the Rose Bedroom), re-covered in the 1850s.

Mahogany washstand, *c.*1830.

Bidet, mahogany, *c.*1850.

Convex circular mirror in gilded frame with dolphins and seahorse, *c.*1820.

The reclining chair, manufactured by John Carter in *c.*1850, is described on its label as a 'Literary Machine' and was, it seems, made for the Library.

CLOCK

Eight-day French striking mantel clock of *c.*1890 with porcelain case and matching urns.

TAXIDERMY

An albino woodcock.

CARPET

English, *c.*1920.

THE CHINESE BEDROOM

A mid-eighteenth-century plan of the house shows this room divided into two. In 1751 the bay window was built by William Windham II and the two rooms united by James Paine, who none the less retained the late seventeenth-century form of coved ceiling. It was described as the 'Bow Window Dressing Room' in 1771, when the Chinese paper hangings would have harmonised beautifully with the white and grey scheme in the adjacent room, which it served. The room then contained, among other things, six mahogany Chinese armchairs, a 'worked' mahogany armchair, a mahogany settee with pillows (perhaps the one in the Yellow Bedroom), a fire-screen with an India (ie Chinese) paper top, a mahogany washstand, a 'Very Fine India Cabinet, Brown and Gilt' (the one now in the Cabinet below) and a Wilton carpet, which was fitted to the room.

The mid-eighteenth-century Chinese wallpaper in the Chinese Bedroom

DECORATION

The 'India paper' hangings (that is Chinese paper ordered through the East India Company), decided on early in 1751, were the subject of much correspondence and delay. Paine was responsible for arranging them and Windham was annoyed that a specialist had to be sent to Felbrigg to fit the sixteen rolls 'at 3s 6d per day while at Felbrigg & 6d per mile travelling charges which I think a cursed deal'. John Scruton, 'the India Paper hanger', worked here and in other rooms between 30 March and 9 May 1752. The effects of many years of damp were repaired in 1974–5, when John Sutcliffe carefully repainted some of the missing areas (eg the pheasant high up to the right of the central window).

FIREPLACE

White marble surround and grate, c.1830.

FURNITURE

Pot cupboard, mahogany, c.1800.

Bed, mahogany, c.1830, but with two posts of c.1750. The chintz hangings are of the later period and match those in the Red Bedroom.

Small Chinese Coromandel lacquer cabinet on fine mid-eighteenth-century English stand, probably the 'Small Elegant India Cabinet in Colours' described in 1771 in what is now the Yellow Bedroom.

A mahogany washstand (see above) with late nineteenth-century Minton bowl and jug.

Two Chinese Chippendale pattern armchairs, c.1750 (see above and also Stair Hall).

A washstand and dressing-table of c.1820.

Mahogany dressing-table glass of c.1790, incorporating cut mirror glass of c.1700.

An unusually small japanned bureau of c.1730 with a mirror door.

The two figures of nodding mandarins on turned brackets are of c.1820, as are the Gothick curtain pelmets here and in the Red Bedroom.

Overmantel mirror, c.1800.

A fine gilded Rococo mirror by John Bladwell, c.1752.

CLOCK

An eight-day French striking mantel clock in a *cloisonné* enamel and ormolu case, by Keen and Page, Paris, c.1910.

THE WEST CORRIDOR

Built in 1751–2 to provide service access to the new bedrooms of the west wing. The water closet at the north end was added by Robert Brettingham in 1788 (see also the Stone Corridor beneath).

PICTURES

FRANK BARNARD (1846–96)
Robert Cooper, a Sheringham fisherman
Watercolour. Signed, dated and inscribed:
Aug. 1870

WALL OPPOSITE WINDOW:

? ENGLISH, ? eighteenth-century
Supposed portrait of Queen Henrietta Maria
Panel
Bought by Ketton-Cremer at the sale of Heydon Hall in July 1949, in the firm belief that it was a portrait of the Queen, though there is nothing to indicate this, and an old label on the back simply calls it: *'A Ladies' Head'*.

ENGLISH, nineteenth-century
Two fishermen by the sea shore

Attributed to NICOLAS-JACQUES JULLIAR
(1719–90)
View of a house and track by a bridge
This picture and its pendant would appear, from their frames, to have been one of the pairs of 'Landskips by Allemand' (Jean-Baptiste Lallemand, 1716–1803) listed in the Drawing Room in 1764 and 1771. Both artists – but particularly Julliar – came under the influence of Boucher, but Lallemand was the better known of the two, so the confusion could easily have arisen.

Studio or Follower of FRANS FRANCKEN II
(1581–1642)
Abraham and Sarah visited by three angels
Panel
The original panel was formed of two planks, but strips of wood have been added subsequently, evidently to make the picture fit the frame, which is of the Drawing Room and Cabinet type. Since this picture is not recorded either in 1764 or 1771, it is evidently a replacement – perhaps of the Berchem. Prime versions of this composition, on copper, are in the Museu de Santa Cruz, Toledo, and in a private collection.

Attributed to NICOLAS-JACQUES JULLIAR
(1719–90)
Watermill and millpond with figures
The pendant of the foregoing picture.

J. SIMON after EDWARD BOWER
(active 1629–d.1666/7)
Two glass engravings of Charles I at his Trial

J. SIMON after JACOPO AMIGONI (c.1682–1752)
The Element of Water
Another glass engraving, but of the kind known as a 'treacle-print', because of the heavy use of brown.

ENGLISH, early nineteenth-century
Two Fishermen and a dog by the sea

ENGLISH, early eighteenth-century
A hunt near Norwich
Evidently once an overmantel picture.

Attributed to JOHN RILEY (1646–91) and
an assistant
Portrait of an Unknown Lady
Riley almost certainly executed the head and hands, but seems to have left the figure and drapery to an assistant. He is known to have collaborated with both J. B. Gaspars and John Closterman in this way.

ENGLISH, eighteenth-century
The Judgement of Paris
This has been attributed to Francis Hayman (c.1708–76), who painted a double portrait of *William Windham II with David Garrick*, but the figures are not really characteristic of him.

Attributed to JOHN RILEY (1646–91) and
an assistant
Portrait of an Unknown Gentleman
The assistant seems to have been less competent than that of its pendant.

ENGLISH, nineteenth-century
The Gypsy Fortune-Teller

SCULPTURE

(*Same circuit*)

DENIÈRE, after an Unknown Sculptor
Equestrian combat of two Gauls
Bronze. Signed: DENIERE
The signature is not that of the sculptor, but of the firm of bronze-founders called Denière, who were active in Paris, father and son, betwen 1818 and the end of the century, chiefly producing furnishing bronzes.

After ANTONIO CANOVA (1757–1822)
Hercules and Lichas
Bronze
The original marble of this celebrated group is in the Galleria Nazionale d'Arte Moderna in Rome.

JOHN CHEERE (1709–87) after LOUIS-FRANÇOIS ROUBILIAC (?1705–62)
Alexander Pope (1688–1744)
Bronzed plaster
From the set on the stairs. Roubiliac's original terracotta is in the Barber Institute, Birmingham, but he also made a number of marble versions.

CHRISTOPHE FRATIN (1800–64)
A lioness bringing her two cubs the corpse of an antelope
Bronze. Signed: FRATIN
The original was exhibited in the Paris Salon of 1835.

FURNITURE

Two mahogany chairs similar in pattern to the walnut chairs in the Great Hall and Stone Corridor, c.1750.

A walnut fall-front bureau of c.1690 with bun feet and inlaid geometrical patterns. Possibly bought by Katherine Windham in 1690/91.

Six handsome mahogany chairs of *c.*1750 with scroll-pattern splats probably from William Windham II's Great Parlour.

A fine mahogany chest-on-chest of *c.*1750.

Two small matching mahogany chests of drawers incorporating a writing surface, *c.*1750.

A mahogany military chest of *c.*1800 with carrying handles, thought to have been used on naval service by Admiral Windham.

A fine burr-walnut chest-on-chest of *c.*1735.

A walnut veneer bureau of *c.*1730–40, doubtless the 'Large Cabinet with Draws Finered, and with a Looking Glass Door' listed in 1771 in the Tapestry Room (over the Morning Room).

Victorian papier-mâché trays by Clay of King Street, Covent Garden.

LIGHTING

The glass bowls on brass pillars are candle shades. The mahogany stands are also for candles and are frequently listed in conjunction with dressing-tables in the 1771 inventory.

CERAMICS

Chinese and English Delft blue-and-white dishes of the eighteenth century.

THE BATHROOM

This room was once a nursery, to judge from the pictorial designs of its early linoleum, and was probably turned into a bathroom by the Ketton-Cremers in the 1920s. Agnes Willoughby, who married 'Mad Windham' for his money in 1861, made clear that she would not move to Felbrigg unless an enamel bath with hot and cold water laid on was installed for her use at the hall. But Wyndham Ketton-Cremer states that there were no bathrooms when his parents moved in, 'since Robert Ketton had remained faithful to the hip-bath all his days'.

FURNITURE

Two important early pieces. A Chinese Coromandel lacquer screen of *c.*1700 and a red lacquer bureau of *c.*1730.

THE BACK STAIRS

The 1680s wing had a service staircase in this area but the present stairs were built in the autumn of 1751. Windham wrote in September, '...talking to Jackson about the turned bannisters for the back stairs, (which Church talked of turning himself as he thinks he can do everything) he says ... he will get them turned and will answer for it that the cheapness shall repay for the carriage by the sea ...' The present ballusters are of a late seventeenth-century type identical to those on the great stairs at Aylsham Old Hall, completed *c.*1686 (see p.16). They must therefore have been salvaged from the demolition of the Felbrigg great stairs, a cheaper solution than the one proposed by Jackson.

THE BIRD CORRIDOR

Built by Admiral Windham in 1831 to improve communication between the Kitchen and Dining Room, this encloses the windows of earlier rooms in the extension built in 1675 (see p.12). In 1734 the first two windows lit the 'Common Drawing Room' (since 1787 the Butler's Pantry), the central one relates to the secondary staircase and in 1734 the furthest window lit the Housekeeper's Room (since *c.*1750 the China Room).

TAXIDERMY

The collection of Thomas Wyndham Cremer (1834–94), the last squire's grandfather, who was a keen ornithologist. The set-ups are by Gunn of Norwich and Pratt of Brighton.

SCULPTURE

The Headless Lady, a figure from an Athenian grave monument of 350–20BC. Part of a large relief which would have included a standing figure on the left-hand side, who was, to judge by other contemporary monuments, probably clasping the seated lady's right hand. There is no record of how this very important ancient Greek sculpture made its way to Felbrigg. It was first recorded at Felbrigg by Grigor, who saw it in the Walled Garden in 1847 and described it as 'A mutilated white marble statue, lately dug up on the plains of Troy'. The figure is a close contemporary of the Elgin Marbles and it may be significant that Philip Hunt, who as chap-

'The Headless Lady', from an Athenian grave monument, 350–20 BC (Bird Corridor)

lain to the Earl of Elgin encouraged the removal of the Parthenon sculptures to England, ended his days as vicar of nearby Aylsham in 1838.

THE BUTLER'S PANTRY

This room, which may be viewed through a pane in the second window on the right, seems to have been fitted out *c.*1787 and was presumably therefore designed by Robert Furze Brettingham for William Windham III. There is a drawing for its cupboarded walls, which would have housed the large quantity of glassware for which the butler was responsible.

THE CHINA ROOM

This room, visible through a pane in the fourth window on the right, was fitted out *c.*1750 with oak cupboards on its east wall and small shelves ranged round the fireplace. Tiled like the one in the Grey Dressing Room, it was fitted with a stove, and now contains a collection of late eighteenth-century blue-and-white plates, bowls and meat dishes. Scratched into one of the lower panes is a verse written in praise of a local beauty, Anne Barnes, by her devoted admirer Benjamin Stillingfleet, William Windham II's tutor (see p.22):

Could Lammy look within my breast
She'd find her image there exprest
In characters as deep as here
The letters of her name appear
And like them ever will remain
Till time shall break my heart in twain.

It is signed 'B. Stillingfleet, fool'. His persistant suit eventually foundered on his lack of income and prospects in 1735 and provoked a *Philippic against Woman*.

THE KITCHEN

The Kitchen has occupied this site since the early eighteenth century, but its ceiling was raised probably *c.*1800, when the two round-headed windows were made in its east wall. The charcoal stove between them is also of this date, but it appears that the old range was removed by the last squire, who introduced the present Aga.

FURNITURE

Two large oak tables, one eighteenth-century, the other Victorian.

Chopping block.

Large oak cupboard, now painted, but originally intended for a more polite room, made *c.*1730 and extended at the back in pine and given a new cornice *c.*1800.

COPPER

Some of the copper is eighteenth-century. It is clear from inventories that it is only part of a rather larger *batterie de cuisine*.

PEWTER

A series of large eighteenth-century chargers, two of which are engraved on their rims with the Windham fetterlock crest.

Part of the batterie de cuisine in the Kitchen

Next to the Kitchen are the doors to the House-keeper's Room and the Still Room.

THE SOUTH CORRIDOR

The new west service wing was built by James Paine for William Windham II in 1749–51 to contain a new Servants' Hall, Steward's Room, a Tenants' Waiting Room and a group of workshops (see p.23). It had lodging rooms on the first floor and an open arcaded walk at the front which was turned into a corridor by W.J. Donthorn in 1825 for Admiral Windham. The colour schemes here and throughout the wing are based on analysis of paint samples and are thought to represent the early nineteenth-century decoration. They were undertaken in 1993.

The fire buckets bear the initials of Rachel Anne Ketton which must have been applied between 1872 (the death of her husband John Ketton) and 1875 (the majority of their son Robert). The leather ones are probably eighteenth-century and their purchase was the subject of anxious letters from the agent Robert Thurston after the explosion of the firework shop in 1755.

FURNITURE

The cupboard with Gothick details is a press provided for William Windham II's library by George Church *c*.1755.

THE SERVANTS' HALL

Before the building of the wing the Servants' Hall was in the west service range. Francis Pank was paid for the floor and ceiling here in November 1749 and George Church received payment 'For fitting up the Servants Hall making the tables benches . . . etc.', which he had undertaken between 27 November and 23 December. He came in again in February 1751 to put up the numerous pegs which line the walls. Church's benches and tables remain in the room. He had also framed the windows here and elsewhere in the wing, and made the heavy doors, which, until the closing-in of the South Corridor, were external.

THE STEWARD'S ROOM

Church fitted out this room between March and May 1750. He was probably also responsible for the handsome oak desk. On 30 January 1752 £1 5s was paid 'for a skin to cover the Desk in the Steward's Room'. The estate was administered from this room until 1970.

PICTURES

ENGLISH, *c*.1780–1800
View northwards over Beeston Regis
Watercolour

CHARLES CATTON the Younger (1756–1819)
Sheringham Beach
Signed and dated: *C Catton Jnr, 1794*
Inscribed on back by Kretton-Cremer: 'I remember my father saying that the figure with the dog and crook (though it is perhaps less like a crook than a boat hook) represents the Shepherd employed at Beeston by my Great Great Grandfather, Cremer Cremer (died 1808), who presumably ordered the picture.'

CLOCK

Eight-day longcase clock by J. Bennet of Norwich, *c*.1780.

THE TENANTS' WAITING ROOM

This room was fitted out by Church in December 1749, but the cupboards at the east end are probably early nineteenth-century.

FURNITURE

Circular mahogany table with drawers and leather top, *c*.1800.

THE TURNERY

This is the name given to this room in the 1771 inventory. It was one of William Windham II's two wood-turning shops. The other one was overhead. George Church set up the 'turns' in November 1750 and in about 1755 Windham made a 29-page inventory of the many and varied contents of the 'upper and lower shops'. There was an impressive array of chisels, differential chucks and other items relating to turning. Windham had Charles Plumier's *L'Art de Tourner en Perfection*, published in Lyon in 1701, with its series of almost impossibly intricate models as well as diagrams of turning apparatus. It was a popular eighteenth-century hobby, though it is unlikely that many country gentlemen were as well equipped as Windham. He had a large range of wood, both hard and soft as well as ivory, tortoiseshell and amber, and had produced at the time of the inventory some little boxes in yew and lignum vitae as well as different types of spinning top. The shops were also used as Windham's arsenal of sporting arms. There were 42 different guns in the upper shop alone, as well as Geneva bows, crossbows, bullet-bows, an Indian ironwood bow and a Madagascar lance.

The upper shop was hung with prints and maps and it was here that Windham had his bookbinding and gilding tools, together with a trunk of manuscripts on Genevan history, which were to find their way into the Library in handsome reverse calf bindings. It is evident that the shops were also used for general joinery work, and there is a list of tools for working iron and brass, for watchmaking and gun repair. On the shelves near the chimney in the lower shop were architectural models, vases, a stile and Italian shutters, while upstairs was a mel of 'ye pigeon house'.

Windham's lists also deal with the Inner and Outward Firework Shops. Their location is uncertain but was perhaps on the north side of the service yard. Paine's plans did not provide for them. The two rooms to the east seem to have been added by William Windham III before 1771.

SURVEYING WHEEL

This eighteenth-century device for measuring distances has a dial calibrated in yards, poles, furlongs and miles, and is marked M. Berge, London. William Windham II was interested in these devices and in 1752 received a slightly preposterous letter from William Cranefield of Sheringham, who, with most elaborate penmanship, began 'Worshipful and Transcendant Sir'. This self-styled 'industrious young tyro' invited Windham's patronage for a newly invented surveying wheel.

FIRE-ENGINE

The house fire-engine was probably provided in the late eighteenth century.

FIREARMS

A spring-gun, late eighteenth-century. A device for discouraging poachers.

A single-barrel sporting rifle, no.8433, by Charles Lancaster, late nineteenth-century.

A single-barrel target shooting bench rifle, late eighteenth-century.

A blunderbuss, by T. Cole, *c*.1670.

A musketoon, by Major Simon Parry, *c*.1680.

A blunderbuss, by Edward Bond, *c*.1770.

A Turkish flintlock rifle, nineteenth-century.

THE KNIFE HOUSE

This room, now used for the reception of visitors, was given this name in 1872 and was a storeroom up to that time.

CHAPTER SEVEN

THE GARDEN AND CHURCH

The gentle south-facing slope, a slightly acid soil and the protection afforded by the Great Wood provide good conditions for gardening at Felbrigg in spite of its notoriously severe climate. Annual average rainfall is 22 inches.

Of the early history of the garden we know very little indeed. One of the earliest references is found in the Green Book of William Windham I, where he records that he enlarged the Parlour Garden (to the west of the house) in 1670.[1] In the late sixteenth-century domestic accounts of Jane Coningsby there is a measured drawing for garden steps but this is annotated in the first William Windham's hand and was probably connected with the alterations of 1670.[2] By the time of his death in 1689 the garden had no doubt assumed the form shown in a plan of 1691 (see p.83), whose limited annotations reveal that the large square of the Parlour Garden lay before the west front, bounded on its southern side by a 'mount walk' or terrace, to the south of which was the flower garden.

Significant changes were made to this arrangement by Ashe Windham following the building of the Orangery (see p.39) during the first decade of the eighteenth century. The Parlour Garden was enlarged and named after the Orangery, 'the Green House Garden', with an elegant curved wall to the west. Although no detail is shown, it would have included some sort of gravel parterre on which the orange trees could be stood out during the summer. The 'Mount Walk', which may have been a very early feature, was removed, presumably to open up a southern view of the Orangery. A new narrow rectangular Parlour Garden with a curved end was laid out to the north of the house. In front of Ashe Windham's south service wing was a square herb garden in whose south-east corner lay the lavatory or 'Necessary House'. Immediately south of the Parlour Garden was the Green Garden and oppo-

site it, south-east of the house, the Orchard. These areas would have been divided by walls and palings, and in the collection there is a drawing for a wrought-iron screen set between hedges which carries Ashe's monogram in the overthrow. A payment to Messrs Montigny and Tijou in 1708 may well be connected with it.[3] In August 1707 Katherine Windham wrote of the garden:

Felbrigg lookt like the land of Goshen so full of everything that was good, abundance of fruit, the peaches not good anywhere this year, but this weather will make them fatter. I eat some excelent green gages, they are admirable, an excelent nectrine that comes from the stone …, excelent white figes, the orenge trees full of large fruit, the Gardner pulled off the blossoms, they bearing too much the year before, that there is few small ones, the vines in the paled yard thrive extreemly, and the trees without the courtyard, my wood is as well as can be expected.[4]

The mid-eighteenth-century plan which records the layout of Ashe's garden is executed in ink but there are also carefully pencilled proposals for planting. In the early part of the century it would have been entirely acceptable for the various service buildings to have appeared in views from the gardens and the house, but as the fashion for natural landscape took hold, such features needed to be artfully concealed. With the loss of the 'Mount Walk' it became necessary to find a way of hiding the coach-house and barns to the south-east from the view of the garden as well as from the southern prospect of the house. So the drawing proposes a belt of planting to enclose these buildings in a sweeping arc on three sides. To the east are two more plantations, one of which engulfs the old dove-house, while the other masks out the southern office range. The only building left out in the open by these plantings was the 'Necessary House'. Ashe's son William Windham II, who may have requested these proposals, built a new necessary house next to the bleaching ground (used for whitening sheets in the sun) on the north side of the hall where this little neo-Jacobean building still stands in a private garden. His agent Robert Frary received precise instructions:

I think it the best place imaginable. Should not the inside be stuccoed, or how do you do it? How many holes? There must be one for a child; and I would have it as light as possible. There must be a good broad place to set a candle on, and a place to keep paper. I think the holes should be wide and rather oblong, and the seats broad and not quite level, and rather low before, but rising behind. Tho the better the plainer, it should be neat.[5]

That William Windham II took trouble over the garden is attested by the expenditure of the vast sum of £655 on Peerson the painter, who decorated palings, posts and rails in front of the house and elsewhere in the garden, several of which had been made by George Church, some to enclose a bowling green.[6] The third William Windham probably continued the process of opening up the south prospect and in 1786 formed a circular carriage sweep before the house.[7] But we know that he did not give much time to Felbrigg once his political career got underway.

THE AMERICAN GARDEN

The garden north of the house and around the Orangery was probably remodelled by Broderick Thomas, who provided a plan in June 1865 for the new owner John Ketton. Many of the trees are of transatlantic origin, notably the American Buckeye (*Aesculus parviflora*) – hence the garden's name. There are also Red Oaks (*Quercus rubra*), False Acacia (*Robinia pseudoacacia*) and the Tulip tree, *Liriodendron tulipiferum*. Wellingtonias (*Sequoiadendron giganteum*) adjoin the Orangery, where they are accompanied by Evergreen Oaks (*Quercus ilex*) and a fine group of the large flowering broom *Genista aetnensis*, next to the path. The remarkable curving trunks of the Western Red Cedars (*Thuja plicata*) make an impressive prelude to the walk which leads to the Walled Garden. It is an altogther typical Victorian pleasure ground, and in recent years the Trust has added summer-flowering rhododendrons and azaleas, bamboo and the flowering privet, *Ligustrum lucidum*.

THE WALLED GARDEN

In 1781 the busy and frequently absent statesman William Windham III leased the vegetable garden to the gardener Nathaniel Brown on condition that he kept it in good order and did not 'alter the Form or Figure of the same on any Account'. A detailed schedule of all its crops, frames and tools was drawn up at the same time.[8]

It is not known when the garden was begun, though William Windham II contributed its most distinctive feature, the octagonal Dove-house, in the early 1750s. The east and west walls were rebuilt by Admiral Windham in 1825 according to the plaque above the entrance. A plan of the garden was made for William Howe Windham in 1834, following the Admiral's death. Grigor's *Eastern Arboretum* of 1847 recorded, 'The Kitchen Garden here is well worthy of notice. It is exceedingly well kept. Through the exertions of Mr Robins of pine growing celebrity, it has been raised to a style of excellence which few gardens present.' W. H. Windham enhanced the ornamental character of the garden, especially of the Dove-house Walk, by introducing the central circular pond and in 1842 the old front-door arch of the hall. The two stone pine-cones on the gateway near the entrance are finials from the roof of the 1680s west wing, taken down in the repairs of 1751. The other smaller pine-cone is a later copy.

During Felbrigg's decline in the early years of this century the Walled Garden was once again leased out, to a market gardener, but there was no investment in the care of its glasshouses. When the last squire's parents took over the property in 1923, they were able to repair only the two main houses on either side of the Dove-house Walk.

The entrance to the garden is flanked by two Irish yews (*Taxus baccata* 'Fastigiata'), planted to match the more mature specimens at the opposite end of the central path, which is defined by the box hedging for which the garden is well known. The gate-piers on the west walk are clad with sweet bays

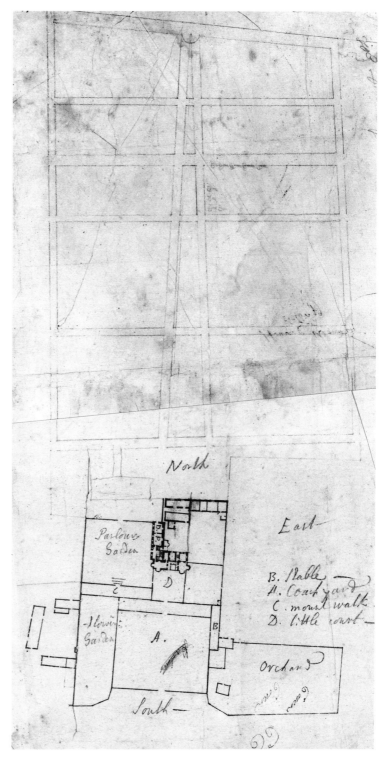

(Above, top) Forcing pots in the Walled Garden

(Above) The Walled Garden

(Right) This plan of 1691 shows the Parlour Garden to the west of the house, separated by a 'mount walk' or terrace from the Flower Garden. The woodland to the north, divided by formal rides, was probably planted by Katherine Windham. The site of the Orangery is indicated in pencil

(*Laurus nobilis*) and myrtles (*Myrtus communis*). Only the north-east section of the garden is still used for vegetables but the walls are well stocked with plums, pears, apples, figs and gages, peaches and nectarines. Among the espaliered apples are early varieties, 'Hubbard's Pearmain' (ie Hobart's and so presumably from Blickling), 'Norfolk Beefing' (pronounced 'Biffin'), 'Lane's Prince Albert' and 'Lady Henniker'. Among the pears there are the seventeenth-century 'Catillac', 'Vicar of Wink-field' and 'Black Worcester'.

The herb border lies to the west of the Dove-house and has become a special feature of the garden during the last decade. The other beds beneath the walls are planted as mixed borders with roses, paeonies, hibiscus, phlox and dahlias. Dahlias were the dominant feature of the central path in the last squire's time but these double borders were re-designed in 1977 by John Sales, the Trust's Gardens Adviser, with a variety of shrubs to provide colour and interest throughout the summer. Planted in front of these in the shelter of the box hedges is

The octagonal Dove-house in the Walled Garden was built in the 1750s

Colchicum tenorei. This colchicum has been at Felbrigg for many years and has more recently become
the focus of a collection of the various forms of the
genus which has quickly become one of the most
comprehensive in any British garden. It has recently
been designated, jointly with the Royal Horti-
cultural Society's garden at Wisley, the National
Collection. Most are established in the north-east
section and can be seen naturalised in grass or lined
out in borders. The north-facing walls are the place
for hostas, the climbing *Hydrangea petiolaris*, lily-of-
the-valley and *Erythronium*.

The central pond is surrounded by lavender
(*Lavandula officinalis* 'Hidcote'), and the island is
planted with *Alchemilla mollis*, or Lady's Mantle.

THE GREENHOUSES

These symmetrical houses appear on the 1834 plan.
One is a vinery with a good specimen of 'Black
Hamburgh' and also contains a grapefruit tree
which fruits regularly. The other is a conservatory
for flowering plants, dominated by a large mimosa
(*Acacia dealbata*).

Near the small propagating house in the north-
west section is a Californian bay (*Umbellularia cali-
fornica*) known, because of its powerfully scented
foliage, as the Headache tree. A good collection of
large old-fashioned roses occupies the plot behind
and others may be seen on the nearby lawn. Either
side of the central path are 'Norfolk Royal Russet'
apples trained as dwarf pyramids. The Orchard area
is left uncut until late summer to allow the wild
flowers to seed.

Thorns and medlars are grown on the lawns in
the central section. The South Lawn is treated as
an open area with attractive cream- and yellow-
flowered climbing roses and various forms of Cean-
othus on its sunny north wall.

THE DOVE-HOUSE

A bill for three days' glaziers' work in the Dove-
house in November 1753[9] probably dates the
building of the present octagon, which has
four semi-circular 'therm' windows of the type
James Paine incorporated into his new service

wing in 1751. In 1923 it was 'almost a ruin, with
gaping holes in the roof, the principal timbers
rotted through, and the cupola leaning drunkenly
awry'.[10] It was restored by Wyndham Ketton-
Cremer in 1937, as the Latin inscription records.
Dove-houses were an important source of meat
in the past and the young birds, or squabs, would
be collected for the kitchen from the numerous
nesting holes.

THE SOUTH GARDEN

This garden, in front of the east wing, was laid out
in memory of Wyndham Ketton-Cremer. Its box-
edged beds contain *Rosa rugosa* 'Fru Dagmar Has-
trup', and Rose 'Nevada' and 'Little White Pet'. On
the south wall of the wing is a fine Wisteria and a
Garrya elliptica.

FELBRIGG CHURCH

St Margaret's church stands about a quarter of a
mile south-east of the hall. Arable farming has long
effaced any sign of the original village of Felbrigg,
which once surrounded it and was probably
deserted in the Middle Ages, but wartime plough-
ing brought up pottery fragments. The building is
mainly late fourteenth-century and much external
masonry of this period survives. In the spandrels of
the west door and on the bases of some of the
buttresses, the carved lion rampant and the fetterlock of the Felbriggs may imply that the church
was rebuilt by Sir Simon Felbrigg (d.1442). Most
of the old windows were renewed in the nineteenth century but original tracery survives in the
blocked windows at the west end of the nave.
There are two medieval porches. The southern
one is the entrance and a lead plaque records the
re-covering of the roofs by the churchwarden
E. Riches in 1732.

The interior is full of interest and character and
perhaps not very much changed since the celebrated
Norwich School painter John Sell Cotman was
married here in January 1809. The nave is given
over to Georgian box pews and the chancel is
dominated by the monuments of the Windhams
(the side windows were blocked to make room for

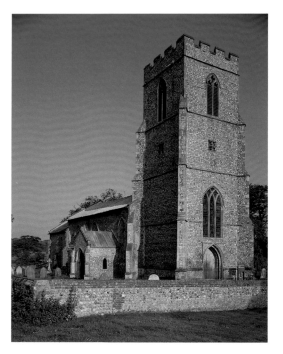

St Margaret's church

them). The earliest tombs are, however, the stone coffin lids on either side of the tower arch, which may be late thirteenth-century. The fine font, decorated with blank tracery, is of *c*.1400 and the cover of 1953 is by Cecil Upcher. The roofs of nave and chancel are good examples of fifteenth-century carpentry.

BRASSES

The church is famous for its monumental brasses, several of which lie in the floor of the nave.

AT WEST END:

A small inscription to *Robert Lounde* (d.1612), and, nearby, *George Felbrigg of Tuttington* (d.1411), an inscription with a decorated quatrefoil which in 1575 still contained the Felbrigg arms, *Or a lion rampant gules*.

TO THE EAST:

The armoured figure of *Thomas Windham* (d.1599), a memorial of 1612 installed by his cousin and heir Sir John Wyndham of Orchard, Somerset, with a powerful inscription typical of the period.

IN CENTRE OF NAVE:

Simon Felbrigg KG, King's Standard Bearer to Richard II (d.1442) and his first wife Margeret (d.1416), a magnificent early fifteenth-century brass set up on the death of Margaret, the daughter of Premyslaus, Duke of Teschen. She was the cousin of Richard II's first queen, Anne of Bohemia. Sir Simon is in plate armour, as was usual for knights of the period, and with the Order of the Garter, the King's standard over his right shoulder.

SOUTH SIDE OF SANCTUARY:

An important brass of *c*.1380 to the grandparents and parents of Sir Simon Felbrigg KG, *Simon de Felbrigg* (d.1351) and *Alice de Thorpe*, *Roger de Felbrigg* (d.1380) and *Elizabeth, daughter of Lord Scales*. Simon is in civilian attire, but his son who, as the inscription relates, died in either Prussia or Paris, was a professional soldier.

IN FRONT OF ALTAR:

The second brass set up by Sir John Wyndham of Orchard in 1612 to *Jane Conyngsby* (d.1608), the sister of Thomas Windham (d.1599, see above).

MONUMENTS

NORTH OF ALTAR:

The earliest is to *Thomas Windham* (1585–1654), the builder of the south front of Felbrigg, and was made by the Norwich mason Martin Morley in 1669 for £45.

ON OPPOSITE SIDE OF CHANCEL AT WESTERN END:

The monument, surmounted by grieving putti, of his successor *William Windham I* (1647–89) and his wife *Katherine* (1652–1729), for which she paid Grinling Gibbons £50 in 1696.

NEXT TO IT:

Two earlier tablets to victims of smallpox, *Joan Windham* (1651/2–69) and *John Windham* (1653–76), both memorials put up by their brother William Windham I and evidently by the same mason. John Windham's tablet cost £21 10s.[11] William Windham's heir, *Ashe Windham* (1673–1749), is the principal subject of the large monument on the north side, possibly by Thomas Carter (see p.25).

His son *William Windham II* (1717–61), had his name and that of his wife *Sarah Lukin* (1710–92) modestly inscribed on the tablet beneath.

SOUTH SIDE OF SANCTUARY:

The Right Hon. William Windham (1750–1810), his famous son, received a grander monument by Nollekens, which was installed in 1813 at a cost of £290 with £30 carriage in front of the beautiful late fourteenth-century sedilia. His widow *Cecilia Forrest* (1750–1824) is commemorated above.

CENTRE OF NORTH WALL:

Windham's successor at Felbrigg, *Vice-Admiral William Lukin* (1768–1833), assumed the Windham name as a condition of his inheritance. Next to his monument is a smaller plaque to his widow *Anne Thellusson* (1775–1849).

NEAR CHANCEL ARCH:

Their eldest son *William Howe Windham* (1802–54), and, above, his widow *Lady Sophia Windham* (1811–63), the daughter of the 1st Marquess of Bristol. She made a controversial second marriage to a young Italian opera singer, Signor Giubilei, in 1858. The son of her first marriage, *William Frederick Windham* (1840–66), the subject of the notorious lunacy inquiry, has a small plaque to the right of Ashe's monument. The monument to his son *Frederick Howe Lindsey Bacon Windham* (1864–96) is below that of Anne Thellusson.

SOUTH SIDE OF NAVE:

Three monuments to members of the Ketton-Cremer family. That of *Robert Wyndham Ketton-Cremer* (1906–69), the historian and last squire of Felbrigg, is nearest the south door, next to the tablets which he put up to his brother *Richard Thomas Wyndham Ketton-Cremer* (1909–41), killed in the Battle of Crete, and their parents *Wyndham Cremer Ketton-Cremer* (1870–1933) and his wife *Emily* (1882–1952).

IN CHURCHYARD:

There are headstones to three important estate servants: Robert Tilstone (d.1675), park keeper, and the two Nicholas Cawstons (d.1846 and 1872), carpenters.

NOTES

1 NNRO, WKC 5/152.

2 NNRO, MF 122.

3 NNRO, WKC 6/23.

4 NNRO, WKC 7/21.

5 NNRO, WKC 7/178/21: January 1752.

6 NNRO, WKC 7/156/9: 1753.

7 NNRO, WKC 7/156/6.

8 NNRO, WKC 7/156/4 and 5.

9 NNRO, WKC 6/43.

10 *Felbrigg*, p.283.

11 NNRO, WKC 5/152.

(Left) The monument to William Windham III (d.1810)

CHAPTER EIGHT
THE PARK AND ESTATE

The estate which Wyndham Ketton-Cremer bequeathed to the National Trust in 1969 consisted of 2,180 acres, of which about a quarter was to be regarded as alienable so that sales could be put towards the endowment. Since then 425 acres of alienable land have been sold; the estate now stands at 1,755 acres.

The nucleus of this estate was built up before the Norman Conquest and enlarged by the Felbrigg family to include a detached holding at Tuttington. Extensive research on the history of the estate by Elizabeth Griffiths has firmly delineated its early development.[1] When Sir John Wyndham acquired Felbrigg in about 1450, he brought with him substantial lands at Wicklewood and Crownthorpe and this holding was increased by his successors, Sir Thomas and Sir Edmund Wyndham, to include land at Sustead and Metton as well as the former monastic property of Beeston Priory. These estates were separated again when the Felbrigg and Tuttington lands were settled by Sir John Wyndham of Orchard on his son Thomas after 1616. Gradual growth in the course of the seventeenth century through the acquisition of a number of smaller holdings was part of a national trend in which the yeoman gradually gave way to the large landowner. During the Civil War estate management suffered from neglect, and when John Windham took over in 1654, he gave over the management to a professional bailiff.

In 1665 William Windham I began an epoch of enterprising direct management whose details were carefully recorded in the famous Green Book (see p.12). Against a background of tumbling corn prices and declining profit margins on fat stock and dairy, however, William Windham's energy only succeeded in averting decline. The increasing wealth which he enjoyed, and which is expressed in the grandeur of his new west wing and the prosperity of Ashe and William Windham II, arose from the clever investment of surplus capital in mortgages and loans. His widow Katherine managed Felbrigg herself from 1689 to 1694, during which time so many tenants gave up in the face of economic recession that she found herself farming nearly half the estate. It was not until Wyndham Ketton-Cremer's inheritance in 1933 that the estate was again managed directly by the family with some professional assistance.

Neither Ashe nor William Windham II were especially interested in land management and the next creative phase was under the aegis of William Windham III. His political career was to give him little leisure and in 1775 he put the estate in the hands of a professional, Nathaniel Kent. With his advice Windham skilfully enclosed much of the common land in the parish, leaving the villagers the least fertile parts of the heath for the gathering of wood. He also bought out one small landowner on very acceptable terms. Felbrigg became a test bed for Kent's theories on the management of timber. He published *Hints to Gentlemen of Landed Property* in 1775, when he had just set about the reorganisation of the woods, and was able to confirm the success of his measures in *A General View of the Agriculture of Norfolk* in 1796. It was at this time that many of the peripheral tree belts were planted and that the general appearance of the park today was established. William Marshall's *Rural Economy of Norfolk*, published in 1787, held up Felbrigg as a model of good management.

The estate reached its largest extent under the improving landlord William Howe Windham, whose initialled date stones bear witness to the great number of farm buildings which he erected or improved throughout the area. In 1854 there were 7,000 acres at Felbrigg together with the newly acquired Hanworth Estate of 1,500 acres, 600 at Alby

View of Felbrigg from the south; watercolour attributed to James Bulwer (1794–1879) (Castle Museum, Norwich)

and a further 1,000 at Dilham, but the repeal of the Corn Laws in 1846 initiated an agricultural recession. At Felbrigg a period of decline was accelerated in the disastrous reign of 'Mad Windham' and finally resulted in the sale of the much reduced estate to John Ketton in 1863. Ketton's son Robert neglected the estate after 1890, but much of this damage was made good by the Ketton-Cremers, who took over in 1924. In the present century there were no further acquisitions and the estate is now one-fifth of its size in 1854. Seven different farms are held by tenants.

THE PARK

The park today divides into two distinct parts, the deep woods to the north (known as the Great Wood) and the area of open parkland to the south of the house. There was a deer-park at Felbrigg in the sixteenth century and its origins were doubtless more ancient. One of the more bizarre legal actions of Roger Wyndham (d.1598) was to bring his wife's nephew before the Court of Star Chamber for killing a deer in Felbrigg park. It is not, however, until the later seventeenth century and the Green Book of William Windham I that we have any details. In 1673 he wrote:

The Park (All but about 30A[cres] behinde my House w[ch] were sowne with severall sorts of Corne) was kept for Deere & to feed sheep for my house my saddle horses and Stranger's horses and 3 Or 4 Cows. Noat I do generally kill about 7 Brace of Bucks and 6 Brace of Does in a yeare. The Meadow was kept for Hay. The Church Close fed with my Cart Horses.[2]

At this stage the Great Wood evidently stood at some distance from the house but it was soon to advance upon it. Until the seventeenth century landowners relied largely on the management of existing indigenous woodland and William Windham I was one of the first to usher in the age of plantations. His copy of the second edition of John Evelyn's *Sylva* of 1670 on practical arboriculture remains in the Library. The experimental character of his plantings, some of which were made unwisely at the height of summer, is indicative of his enthusiasm. In 1676 he noted:

I paled the Nurserye (which I hope will be carefully preserved so long as it please God to continue it in the ffamily). & did then sow there 6 Comb of Acorns: 1 Comb of Ashe Keys: 1 Comb of Haws: 2 bushells of Holly: Berryes: 1500 Chestnuts: 1 bushell of Maple & Sycamore Keys; 7 a very few Beech Mast. I did then plant 4000 Oakes: 800 Ashes: 600 Birches: 70 Beeches: 7 50 Crabs wch were all small. Sr H. Bedingfeld gave me the Oaks: Sr John Potts the Ashe & Birch. The Beech came from Edgefield.[3]

The Nursery, carefully tended by Gotts the gardener, was used to stock the new plantations: 'I enlarged the wood from the 3^d Cross Walk to the Wall and planted it with trees of my sowing. Anno 1676. And 1000 Birches which Sr H. Hobart gave me 6 De^br 1687.' The Nursery also supplied trees for a three-acre plantation taken out of 'Tompson's farm' in 1679 and so that he could make a copse for the deer near the Aylmerton Gate in 1681. The trees seem to have been planted in regular patterns, as in the mixed plantation of walnuts, chestnuts, oaks and limes, where he noted 'the 49 stand square 7 every way'. That his neighbours were engaged in similar activities is evident from these remarks and from a note of 1678: 'I planted the trees on the West side of the fflower Garden which Mr Earle gave me out of Cawston Nurserye.'[4]

It is sad that we have no maps from the period to illustrate Windham's planting. Where, one wonders, was the much-loved Nursery? At the lower edge of an important mid-eighteenth-century plan of the house and its surroundings are two narrow pieces of land called the 'Nursery Slips', which could indicate that it lay directly in front of the house and adjoined them. Such a prominent position would explain Windham's hopes for its longevity. The little plan of 1691 (see p.83) shows an ambitious woodland layout to the north of the hall covering much of the area which Windham described as 'sowne with severalle sorts of Corne'. This part is drawn in red chalk and was presumably the proposal for which the plan was made. The 30 per cent drop in corn prices in 1689, the year of Windham's death, could well have prompted this grand new planting

by his widow Katherine, and what remains of it today is represented by the ragged old sweet chestnuts to the north of the house. She established another, as yet unlocated, new wood in 1728, a year before her death, when she wrote to Ashe:

I have been very busy directing the new wood, we have planted 4,200 Chestnuts, 300 Beeches, 300 Birches, sowed 3 Bushels of acorns, & some Hawes and they tell me it makes a preety figure so I please myself in time to come as you ride by you will remember me & live to reap some profit of it.[5]

The Great Wood was progressively enlarged during the course of the next two centuries, and anyone who walks through it today will soon come across the series of three long sickle-shaped banks which represent its expanding northern boundary in the late seventeenth century, in 1777 under William Windham III, and in 1826. William Windham I planted conifers as well as deciduous trees. There was extensive planting of 'Scotch firs' in July 1682, when he lined the Pond Walk with some that he had sown himself and some acquired from Sir John Hobart of Blickling.[6] The Pond is probably the present lake, which until 1830 still had two old rectangular fishponds at its northern end.

Firs were also a feature of a distinctive clearing, which was already a well-established feature when Humphry Repton described it for Armstrong's *History of Norfolk* in 1781:

In the centre of the Great Wood is an irregular oval of about four acres surrounded by a broad belt of lofty silver firs. On entering this oval the eye is wonderfully pleased, without at first perceiving why it is so; we suppose it must be from the contrasts which this sameness of green makes to the varied tints of the other forest trees, everywhere mixed in the rest of the grove, and which these lofty evergreens entirely exclude.

The eighteenth century at Felbrigg is chiefly remarkable for the plantations of William Windham III, undertaken by Nathaniel Kent. Between 1770 and 1788 he made more than thirteen different new plantations, some of them no more than clumps, others extensive belts and woods. They included in 1778 the Marble Hills Clump, the Church Close Plantations and the Triangle Plantation, in 1779 the Church Circle, in the 1780s plantings west of Round Wood, the wood near the Mustard Pot, Sexton Wood and much else besides. This work was contemporary with Humphry Repton's period at Sustead and his employment as Windham's secretary. It is quite conceivable that he was in some way involved, even though he had yet to begin his career as a professional landscape designer. But if that was so, he never acknowledged it in his later publications. The fact remains, however, as John Phibbs has shown,[7] that the park is Reptonian in character, with its gracefully sculpted clumps and belts, and the ingeniously meandering approach from the Marble Hills to the south-east, which in the eighteenth century gave visitors the best possible impression of the scale and natural beauty of the park without taking them much out of their way. Even the whitewashing of the hall which is remarked upon in Craven Ord's journal, and which must have helped it stand out in the long view from the Marble Hills, was something which Repton was to recommend to his clients in later years. The enlargement of the parkland at this period is commemorated in Admiral Windham's splendid map of 1830, which shows in the vicinity of the church and elsewhere lines of trees that are clearly old field boundaries.

There are surprisingly few ornamental park buildings, but the accounts speak of a temple and amongst the drawings there are designs for an ornamental cottage in the woods similar in conception to the late eighteenth-century cottage which Repton designed for Lady Buckinghamshire in the Great Wood at Blickling. All that survives in Felbrigg's Great Wood is a Gothick ice-house (see below). One major building swept away by William Howe Windham was the old parsonage, or Felbrigg Cottage, as it became known, which stood south-east of the road junction at Park Farm and had been his father's home before he inherited Felbrigg. This charming Georgian building had a great vegetable garden scarcely smaller than the present Walled Garden and its removal opened up the view on the approach from Cromer. The woods and the parkland were much neglected at the close of the nineteenth century and remained so until the Ketton-Cremers arrived in 1924. They planted very large numbers of trees and at the end of the

Rick-building on the Felbrigg estate in the late nineteenth century

Second World War Wyndham Ketton-Cremer celebrated the allied victory with a V-shaped plantation behind the house, one of whose arms frames the very distant prospect of the spire of Norwich Cathedral.

The Trust has continued Ketton-Cremer's woodland management and in recent years worked with its agricultural tenants in a scheme to put down to grass areas of the park that have for many years been in arable cultivation.

ESTATE BUILDINGS

THE CROMER LODGES

The twin neo-Jacobean lodges which form the Victorian main entrance to the estate were built northeast of the house by William Howe Windham in 1841 to designs by G. and J. C. Buckler (see p.31).

THE MARBLE HILL LODGES

These two buildings flank the late eighteenth-century main park entrance south-east of the house and were probably built in the 1840s. Noticeably different in scale and treatment from the Cromer Lodges, they resemble a drawing in the hand of John Adey Repton and watermarked 1845. An avenue which cuts across the farmland (now outside the estate) gave additional emphasis to this entrance.

THE KEEPER'S COTTAGE

Another lodge at the southern extremity of the park, which, like the Marble Hill lodges, resembles a John Adey Repton drawing of c.1845. No longer part of the estate.

MUSTARD POT COTTAGE

Shown on Admiral Windham's estate map of 1830, this lodge marked the eastern entrance and the drive ran in front of it until the building of the Cromer Lodges in the following decade.

SEXTON'S LODGE

A neo-Jacobean lodge built for John Ketton. His initials and the date 1864 adorn the western gable. Extended to the east by Peter Cleverley in 1974.

HALL FARM, FELBRIGG

A late eighteenth-century farmhouse due east of the hall. The farm buildings are partly the work of Admiral Windham (the barn of 1832), but there are several from 1837 onward put up by William Howe Windham.

HALL FARM, METTON

Originally an early seventeenth-century building (see Hall Farm Cottages below), whose west gable wall survives. Extended in English-bond brickwork at the eastern end in the late seventeenth century and then partially refronted in brick in the eighteenth century. The farm buildings were rebuilt in the 1840s, some of them bearing William Howe Windham's date stones. The site is surrounded by the remains of an ancient moat.

ICE-HOUSE

The bricks are of a late seventeenth-century size and type and one of them is dated 1633, although the Gothick detailing suggests the eighteenth century. It may have been built of bricks from a demolished section of the seventeenth-century park wall. The shaft is 28 feet deep.

HALL FARM COTTAGES, METTON

Three cottages made out of a substantial farmhouse of 1608, which now comprises the southern three and a half bays. The west elevation and south gable have the pedimented window heads typical of Norfolk's early seventeenth-century architecture, as distinct from the 'imported' style of Felbrigg's slightly later south front.

PARK FARM

No longer part of the estate but originally one of the most important farmsteads with a large range of buildings put up by William Howe Windham during the 1830s and '40s.

PARK WALL

The earliest reference to the wall is the contract in November 1641 between Thomas Windham and Robert Allne of Antingham for 'three hundred yards in length of seven foot and half highe'. Allne was

The tenants of Park Wall Farm in the late nineteenth century

to be paid four pence per square yard and Allne was to allow Wyndham a month's work in recompense for absenting himself from the harvest in the previous year.[8] There was more work on the wall later in the century.

SUSTEAD

On the south-west edge of the estate. Patrick St Clair, Ashe Windham's tutor and rector of Aylmerton and Sustead, is commemorated by a black marble slab in the fine Decorated church. He lived at Sustead Old Hall, the house with the twin, stepped gables south-west of the church, until his death at 96 in 1755. Humphry Repton was another resident in the 1770s and '80s, when he was happily 'obliged to enact the various parts of churchwarden, overseer, surveyor of the highways, and esquire of the parish'.[9]

NOTES

1 Elizabeth Griffiths, 'The Management of Two Norfolk Estates in the Seventeenth Century: Blickling and Felbrigg 1596–1717', unpublished PhD thesis, University of East Anglia, 1987.

2 NNRO, WKC 5/152.

3 Ibid.

4 Ibid.

5 NNRO, WKC 7/21.

6 NNRO, WKC 5/152.

7 J. L. Phibbs, 'A Reconsideration of Repton's Contributions to the Improvements at Felbrigg, Norfolk, 1778–84', *Garden History*, xiii, 1, spring 1985, pp.33–44.

8 NNRO, WKC 5/420. Quoted in J. L. Phibbs, *Felbrigg Park: A Survey of the Landscape*, 1982.

9 See Carter, Goode and Laurie, *Humphry Repton, Landscape Gardener*, 1983, p.9.

BIBLIOGRAPHY

The family papers are held at the Norfolk and Norwich Record Office, the architectural drawings at the house.

AMYOT, T., *Speeches in Parliament of the late Right Honourable W. Windham, with some Account of his Life*, 1813.

BACK, D. H. L., 'Firearms at Felbrigg', *National Trust Studies*, 1979, pp.51–9.

BARING, Mrs Henry, ed., *The Diary of the Right Hon. William Windham*, 1866.

BARTELL, E., *Cromer Considered as a Watering Place*, 2nd ed. 1806.

BLOMEFIELD, F., *History of Norfolk*, viii, 1805, pp.107–18.

CLABBURN, Pamela, 'A Countryman's Wardrobe: Costume at Felbrigg Hall, Norfolk', *Country Life*, 18 December 1980, pp.2344–5.

COOK, B., 'The Headless Lady of Felbrigg Hall', *National Trust Studies*, 1980, pp.133–140.

CORNFORTH, John, 'Felbrigg Hall, Norfolk', *Country Life*, 5 April, pp.138–41; 12 April 1990, pp.102–5.

FORD, Sir Brinsley, 'Staying at Felbrigg as a Guest of Wyndham Ketton-Cremer', *National Trust Yearbook*, 1977–8, pp.52–62.

GRIFFITHS, Elizabeth, 'The Management of Two Norfolk Estates in the Seventeenth Century: Blickling and Felbrigg 1596–1717', unpublished PhD thesis, University of East Anglia, 1987.

HAWCROFT, F. W., 'The "Cabinet" at Felbrigg', *Connoisseur*, May 1958.

KENT, Nathaniel, *Hints to Gentlemen of Landed Property*, 1775; *A General View of the Agriculture of Norfolk*, 1796.

KETTON-CREMER, R. W., *The Early Life and Diaries of William Windham*, 1930; 'Felbrigg Hall', *Country Life*, 22 December 1934, pp.666–71; *The Church of St Margaret, Felbrigg*, 1st ed., 1935; *Norfolk Portraits*, 1944; 'Johnson's Last Gifts to Windham', *The Book Collector*, 1956; *Norfolk Assembly*, 1957; *Country Neighbourhood*, 1951; *Felbrigg: The Story of a House*, 1962; 'A Note on Thomas Windham', *Norfolk Archaeology*, xxxii, pp.50–2.

LASCELLES, Mary, 'Robert Wyndham Ketton-Cremer 1906–1969', *Proceedings of the British Academy*, lvi, 1970, p.403f.

LEACH, Peter, *James Paine*, 1988.

MACANDREW, D., 'Mr and Mrs Windham: A mid-Victorian melodrama from real life', *The Saturday Book*, 1951.

MACKIE, M., *Cobwebs and Cream Teas*, 1983.

MILNER, John, 'Sir Simon Felbrigg, KG: The Lancastrian Revolution and Personal Fortune', *Norfolk Archaeology*, xxxvii, pp.84–91.

O'DONNEL, Rory, 'W. J. Donthorn (1799–1859): Architecture with "great hardness and decision at the edges"', *Architectural History*, xxi, 1978, pp.83–92.

PHIBBS, John, 'Felbrigg Park: A Survey of the Landscape', unpublished report for the National Trust, 1982; 'A Reconsideration of Repton's Contributions to the Improvements at Felbrigg, Norfolk, 1778–84', *Garden History*, xiii, 1, spring 1985, pp.33–44.

TUDOR-CRAIG, Algernon, *The Lukin Family*, 1932.

WADE-MARTINS, P., 'The Archaeology and Landscape Features of the Felbrigg Estate, Norfolk', unpublished report prepared for the National Trust.

WADE-MARTINS, S., 'Vernacular Farm Buildings of the Felbrigg Estate', unpublished survey for the National Trust.

WATERSON, Merlin, 'The Shipwright Squire?' and 'Brigantines and Battlepieces' [Marine pictures at Felbrigg Hall], *Country Life*, clxxx, 1986, pp.438–40, 904–6.

WILSON, W. D., 'National Trust Vernacular Buildings Survey: Felbrigg Estate', 1992, unpublished.

WOODFORDE, Christopher, *The Norwich School of Glass Painting in the Fifteenth Century*, 1950, pp.20–30.

WYNDHAM, H. A., *A Family History, 1410–1688: The Wyndhams of Norfolk and Somerset*, 1939.

INDEX

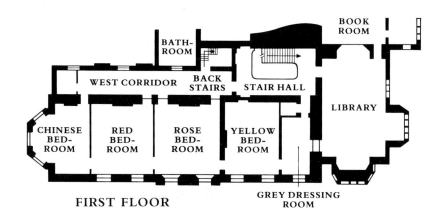

FIRST FLOOR

BATH-ROOM

BOOK ROOM

WEST CORRIDOR

BACK STAIRS

STAIR HALL

LIBRARY

CHINESE BED-ROOM

RED BED-ROOM

ROSE BED-ROOM

YELLOW BED-ROOM

GREY DRESSING ROOM